ARTIFICIAL INTELLIGENCE TECHNIQUES IN LANGUAGE LEARNING

ELLIS HORWOOD SERIES IN COMPUTERS AND THEIR APPLICATIONS

Series Editor: IAN CHIVERS, Consultant to the Monitoring and Assessment Research Centre, London and formerly Senior Programmer and Analyst, Imperial College of Science and Technology, University of London

Series continued at back of book

ARTIFICIAL INTELLIGENCE TECHNIQUES IN LANGUAGE LEARNING

R. W. LAST, BA, MA, PhD, FRSA
Head of Department of Modern Languages
University of Dundee

ELLIS HORWOOD LIMITED
Publishers · Chichester

Halsted Press: a division of
JOHN WILEY & SONS
New York · Chichester · Brisbane · Toronto

First published in 1989
ELLIS HORWOOD LIMITED
Market Cross House, Cooper Street,
Chichester, West Sussex, PO19 1EB, England
The publisher's colophon is reproduced from James Gillison's drawing of the ancient Market Cross, Chichester.

Distributors:

Australia and New Zealand:
JACARANDA WILEY LIMITED
GPO Box 859, Brisbane, Queensland 4001, Australia

Canada:
JOHN WILEY & SONS CANADA LIMITED
22 Worcester Road, Rexdale, Ontario, Canada

Europe and Africa:
JOHN WILEY & SONS LIMITED
Baffins Lane, Chichester, West Sussex, England

North and South America and the rest of the world:
Halsted Press: a division of
JOHN WILEY & SONS
605 Third Avenue, New York, NY 10158, USA

South-East Asia
JOHN WILEY & SONS (SEA) PTE LIMITED
37 Jalan Pemimpin # 05–04
Block B, Union Industrial Building, Singapore 2057

Indian Subcontinent
WILEY EASTERN LIMITED
4835/24 Ansari Road
Daryaganj, New Delhi 110002, India

© **1989 R. W. Last/Ellis Horwood Limited**

British Library Cataloguing in Publication Data
Last, R. W. (Rex William), *1940–*
Artificial intelligence techniques in language learning. —
(Ellis Horwood series in computers and their applications).
1. Artificial intelligence related to language
I. Title
006.3

Library of Congress card no. 89–33533

ISBN 0–7458–0177–3 (Ellis Horwood Limited)
ISBN 0–470–21503–8 (Halsted Press)

Typeset in Times by Ellis Horwood Limited
Printed in Great Britain by Hartnolls, Bodmin

Table of contents

1

Setting the scene

1.1 INTRODUCTION

Let me begin by making it clear whom I am not writing for. This book is not written by an artificial intelligence (AI) expert for the benefit of other AI experts. The specialist literature in the field is already vast and growing rapidly, and I leave it to others far better qualified than I am to add to that body of knowledge.

Nor is this a campaigning manifesto by someone convinced of the reality of AI and the achievability of its goals within the framework of the current state of technology as it applies to computer-assisted language learning (CALL). My approach has been one of cautious inquiry in an area of investigation in which almost as much effort appears to have been expended in the debate between proponents of radically different perceptions of what AI can (and in the views of some ought to be allowed to) achieve as in producing the actual research work itself. Still, it is not surprising that an attempt to clone the human brain onto a machine, as it were, should give rise to a heated scientific debate in a field which is as fraught with potential conflict and moral dilemmas as that of genetic engineering.

What has fuelled my own growing concern about AI is that, unlike the geneticists, who are asking whether achievable goals should be attained on ethical or other grounds, AI researchers, as well as posing themselves such questions, are also asking whether the goal itself is achievable at all. Even given a huge amount of computing power, it may well be that the workings of the human mind still cannot be modelled on any computing machine that we can currently envisage, not least because the way in which the mind functions is still very much a mystery to us, and, as at least one leading researcher has proposed, may well always remain a mystery. If those workings are ever fully understood, it may well prove necessary to devise a quite different order of computing machine to emulate them, perhaps even a computer based on living cells. But the challenges do not end there — even if the human mind yielded up every last secret of its functionings, there would still remain intractable difficulties to be resolved, in that the mind does not function in isolation, but in relation to problem domains of huge complexity, from, say, driving a car to predicting the future path of weather systems.

Indeed, if I had been given to grand subtitles, I would have been tempted to give this study the subtitle *The road to disillusionment,* since I set off to research this book with the near conviction that in AI there lay ready and waiting the potential for a real advance in CALL, but the more I read and hopefully understood, the greater my recognition became that, far from being near the goal (whether desirable or not) of creating a mechanical likeness of the human mind in all its complexities, research is really only just beginning to chip away at the enormously challenging problems that face workers in this field, whether they are involved in 'pure' AI, seeking to model the human mind, or 'applied' AI, attempting to create computerized emulations of intelligent behaviour.

As we shall see, such advances as there have been are in areas where the problem is well-defined and its elements static and transparent. In other areas, it is evident that we are making only the first faltering steps in the direction of AI, and it is equally becoming clear that the goal of mimicking the brain on a computer may well not be attainable at all, given the complexity, instability, and unpredictable interaction between a vast number of parameters that characterize many of the real-world problem domains which we seek to understand and control. In addition, there is a growing voice of caution to be heard among researchers into the ways in which the artificially intelligent computer may well be impoverishing the workplace and deskilling the workforce, and also posing a threat in general to our human qualities and needs. There appears to be a real danger of the marginalization of humanity in favour of the intelligent machine.

These are, of course, very big issues indeed, and the reader may well ask how such wide-ranging concerns impact on the narrow field of CALL and AI. The more I have considered the subject and the implications of involving AI-like techniques in language skills acquisition, however, the more convinced I have become that it is essential for the language teacher employing advanced technology of this kind to be aware of those issues, and of the dangers they threaten as well as the promises they hold out to improve and enhance language teaching. Indeed, in my view the real danger lies in the opposite, reductionist stance, in which individual researchers concentrate on ever narrower specialisms without removing their heads from the sand to scan the intellectual horizon. It has been argued that such attitudes are responsible for an uncontrolled drift in the direction of AI without the long-term implications beyond immediate 'gains' being fully thought out and recognized.

In addition, the pressure towards 'progress' in information technology and its related fields has never been stronger, not only in the scientific world, but in our own field of modern languages, too, where chalk and talk have over recent decades given place first to the language laboratory, then the television set, the video recorder, now the microcomputer, and potentially in the future the intelligent tutoring system. To have been in the vanguard of these advances is regarded as a positive, career-enhancing achievement, but those who have voiced caution and concern about the negative aspects of new technologies have tended to be dismissed as inflexible, old-fashioned and incapable of withstanding the shock of the new. And in modern languages, the lure of the new technology has never been stronger, not just in the recruitment of computing and other technologies in the transmission of language skills to our own traditional cohorts of students, but also in the rapidly developing growth — more in public-sector higher education than in the universities — of courses in which languages are linked with office and business skills, and even with computer studies themselves, both at undergraduate and at postgraduate level. And such developments are equally taking place in the secondary schools.

The fact that a growing number of modern languages students are now not only 'computerate', in the general sense of having been exposed to computers in other disciplines, but are actually using computing equipment in foreign language word processing, information retrieval from library systems, and so forth is an additional pressure point. The students themselves are increasingly beginning to expect a high profile for the computer in a go-ahead modern languages department, again at both secondary and tertiary levels.

In addition, of course, there is the pressure emanating from the EEC for the development of language courses in which new technologies seem tailormade to fit the requirements. The EEC, too, is highly conscious of the significance of technology-based research and development, and it has established an expensive long-term machine translation project, Eurotra, to assist in the translation of the documentation mountain among the various languages of the growing body of the community.

Given all these pressures, then, it seems inevitable that modern language teachers, having taken the initial step with CALL, should embrace these new developments and welcome their assistance in the highly labour-intensive and expensive business of teaching modern languages at its various levels and for a growing range of different specialist purposes. That, indeed, was my motivation for exploring the potential impact of AI upon CALL, and that was why I set about writing this book, to pass on to others what little I had learned about how best to target the impact of AI on CALL. But the more I investigated, the more my doubts grew about the course which we appear to be embarking on. I do not simply mean that computers are inappropriate tools in language teaching. There is more than enough evidence, from my own work and from the researches of others, that the computer has a significant and growing role to play.

What I am anxious to warn against is taking a headlong rush in this new direction, as did the early researchers into CALL, myself included, without stepping back and considering the wider implications as well as the immediate practicalities. The issues are huge and very complex, and I hope only to have made an initial step in the direction of coming to grips with them. So what started off in life as a workshop manual for AI in CALL has turned out to be a quite different book indeed.

1.2   THE TASK BEFORE US

My objective, then, is to examine, from the point of view of the informed modern languages teacher and researcher, the current developmental level of CALL, to try and disentangle the present state of the art of AI as it may relate to CALL, and to seek to establish the extent to which AI applications can — or should — be applied to the future development of CALL. In addition, I shall be considering the broader implications raised by these issues.

Throughout, I have used the acronym CALL as a synonym for the American CALI (computer-assisted language instruction), rather than other contenders like CBL (computer-based learning), and so forth, on the grounds that CALL is a perfectly adequate umbrella term and that the fine distinctions implied by other variants add nothing constructive to the discussion of the issues concerned.

In this study, I am also taking my cue from researchers like Cameron, who points the direction in the introduction to papers from the 1985 conference in the University of Exeter on *The computer and post A-level modern language teaching:*

> In the short term, this book reveals what use, in spite of the limitations of the hardware available, can be made of the computer *now*. And yet, it may be that the real future lies in Artificial Intelligence. As one reads through the chapters in this book, one realizes that much has been achieved and that much more will be achieved by selecting ideas which have been tried out by individuals and by amalgamating them. (Cameron *et al.*, 1986, p. 11.)

It is my purpose to try and establish the validity of Cameron's speculation that AI 'may be' the way forward, and if so, how best the challenge of the new approach should be met.

1.3 THE BALANCE OF CONTENT

The computer scientist reading the pages that follow might well feel that the balance is wrong, that too much knowledge is assumed in some places, and too little in others. He or she — or indeed any other reader from outside the language-teaching community — should, however, bear in mind the fact that the readership that I am writing for has a very different kind of profile from that of the mathematician, computer programmer, or indeed any kind of scientist.

To borrow a term from AI, the average language teacher's 'world knowledge' in relation to such subject areas as expert systems, the history of AI, the significance or otherwise of ELIZA, SHRDLU, the GPS, and a string of other topics is not likely to be very substantial, nor is there any reason why it should be so. This implies that in such areas a greater measure of explanation and exposition will be required. But in other subject areas, such as grammar, syntax, and the messily ambiguous and complex nature of knowledge about language — here the language teacher has a distinct advantage over his scientific counterpart, and I shall be able to make assumptions that those areas are well known to the reader.

But this does not mean that the language teacher is wholly unfamiliar with computers and computing. Indeed, it is highly likely that the secretarial office will have computing equipment to cope with the increasing through-put of documentation required in language teaching, and equally that the teacher will have personal access to word processing, spreadsheet and other applications packages. In addition, many will have either purchased CALL material and employed it in real teaching situations, or they may even have developed and produced their own computer-based material.

Although computers have now become firmly established in modern languages departments, both as teaching aids, as well as in the role of word processors, and tools in text and information processing and indeed in publishing itself, it was as a CALL machine that the computer made its first significant impact among language teachers. But in the early days of humanities computing, from the 1950s onwards, computers meant main-frame computers, usually located in university computing centres.

1.4   THE EARLY DAYS

The mainframe machines of that era were hugely expensive, of varying degrees of reliability, and in the first decade or so offered an interaction with the user which would be regarded today as risibly primitive. The first programs I wrote were clattered out on a card punch (at least we had electric punches, and did not have to hand-punch the code and data), the deck of cards was submitted to reception, and the turn-round time between runs of a program in development could characteristically be counted in hours. If the machine crashed, hours could extend into days.

Given that modality of interaction, it was hardly to be wondered at that the language teacher saw no possibility of applying this unreliable electronic monster in the teaching process, and it would have been unremarkable if language teachers and humanities researchers as a whole had dismissed the computer out of hand as a purely scientific instrument with limited addi-tional potentiality in the world of commerce as an accounting and payroll tool. I shall be considering the early attempts at mechanical translation later; here I am concerned with the principal developments in the UK.

But it was not the case that humanists ignored the computer. Isolated pioneers began to recognize that the speed with which even in those days the computer could manipulate data had a potentially very powerful role to play in areas of quantitative linguistic and literary research. So it was that natural language text began to be fed into the computer, and concordances, stylistic analyses, textual profiles, studies in disputed authorship, and much more appeared in the literature.

In those areas a steady, if limited, advance in knowledge has been recorded over the years in the publications of the Association for Literary and Linguistic Computing (ALLC) and journals such as *Computing and the Humanities*. In addition, packages for textual analysis began to appear, beginning with the pioneering COCOA program, and culminating in its successor the OCP (Oxford Concordance Program). Over the years, the ALLC, which began with a surprisingly broad international base in countries as diverse as Norway, Italy, and the USA, has grown into the leading organization worldwide in this field, and works in collaboration with other groupings of scholars, notably in the ACH (Association for Computing in the Humanities) to promote humanities computing and provide a forum and platform for the presentation and discussion of research in this now rapidly advancing field.

When the days of 'cards in, line-printer paper out' gradually yielded place to the beginnings of on-line interaction in a multi-user environment, it was recognized that, even given the limitations of poor response times, uncertain reliability and operating systems designed for the expert rather than the naive user, here existed a potential for CALL. An early paper of mine reminds me just how complex the challenge of devising a user interface was in the 1970s:

> Each learner is given a copy of the handout *How to use the EXERCISE macro* which, in conjunction with a 15-minute video-tape demonstration, teaches him about the package within a very short space of time. Having plucked up courage to go to a console, the majority of learners make meaningful progress with the package within a matter of minutes. Once logged in under a special user-name, the learner is protected against the system in that he is limited in the number of commands he is permitted to use.... The EXER-CISE macro itself is both self-explanatory and has comprehensive error diagnostic facilities in the event of a student mistyping the name of an exercise, or forgetting which exercises are available, etc. (Last, 1979, p. 166.)

It all seems terribly primitive and unwieldy now, but in those days the notion of a lecturer from a languages department booking the console room for an hour a week in order to teach German was quite unheard of, and caused a great deal of interest and curiosity on the part of the scientists who thought the computer was their exclusive province.

So early investigations established that the potential existed for CALL, but that the current technology was being stretched to its limits and beyond, not just on the level of robustness of interaction, but also in the absence of such equipment as visual display units with foreign-language accented characters and other facilities. When the great leap forward of the micro-computer became a reality, many more enthusiasts tackled the challenge of CALL, but for a variety of quite understandable reasons the initial leap forward into the computerizing of some aspects of the language-teaching process has not measured up to its early promise. No really significant advances appear to have been made over the early programs, and in fact some of the material available today, stripped of its colours, accents and other surface attributes, bears a striking resemblance in its essential features to the very earliest work recorded in the literature.

1.5   THE LACK OF ADVANCE IN CALL

CALL has generally not made any real advance beyond a fairly modest level of sophistication, although computing technology has marked up considerable advances over the last decade or so. In addition, programming techniques and languages have improved beyond recognition, and so too has our knowledge of data storage and retrieval techniques and many other fields of potential relevance to CALL. Yet CALL itself seems to be held back in its development.

There are two very straightforward factors which help to explain why this is so. The first is that any new field of research activity demands a certain irreducible amount of time and research input before it attains what might be called 'escape velocity'. In other words, people new to CALL are still entering the field without there being a sufficiently large body of research and advancement for them to feel that they have to undertake a lengthy period of study before they can make their own input to the subject. The pioneering spirit is still very much abroad, and from meetings I have addressed it is very clear that the majority of language teachers in the higher education field still know relatively little about the subject. In conferences in the early 1980s, there was much talk of avoiding the reinvention of the wheel, and it is significant that even in late 1988, in the document announcing the launch of a new international journal *Computer Assisted Language Learning*, this phrase is still continuing to be employed:

> It has become apparent from conferences we have organized at Exeter, and elsewhere, and from correspondence with colleagues at home and overseas, that it is essential that there be an easily accessible means of information distribution about current research and its findings. We have to avoid the 'reinvention of the wheel' syndrome.

This awareness of the need to provide a broad basis for genuine advance has been equally apparent to me in my role as Specialist Chairman for CALL in the ALLC, and is one of the motivational forces behind this book.

There is, however, another reason — not a crucial one, but one that should not be overlooked — why there has been a lack of a considerable forward thrust in CALL away from the very basic kind of material which is presently available. The reason is this: many researchers have found that a limited knowledge of a programming language such as BASIC, coupled with a measure of ingenuity and a relatively modest input of time and effort, can produce straightforward programs, mainly of the tutorial type, which the learners find extremely valuable and rewarding despite their evident technical shortcomings. Because the educational value of such CALL packages appears so evident to their creators, and because too they are fully aware of the steepness of the learning curve towards more sophisticated programs together with the uncertainty of gaining any significant benefit when straying away from an uncomplicated question and answer environment, there has been a readily understandable tendency to steer clear of such challenges and stay with material of proven, if limited, worth and value.

But, those reasons apart, the prime cause for a lack of advance in CALL is in my estimation the fact that CALL researchers have not really begun to assimilate the research work that has been done and which continues to grow in quantity and potential relevance, and it was this factor which was one of the key reasons that led me to put this book together. I felt it was no longer satisfactory to approach the computer from an 'amateur' viewpoint (in the sense of the enthusiast who has no thorough theoretical grounding in the equipment he is applying), but to attempt to explore as far as possible the advances in computing in a widely diverse range of fields which might have some relevance to an attempt to give a new initiative to CALL. And, almost inevitably, it was the vast amount of research and development in the field of AI which provided the main source of interest and attraction.

Having ploughed through as much of the literature as I could master, it is even more evident now to me why so relatively few CALL researchers have attempted to move forward. The material is so diverse — some couched in technical language requiring an advanced understanding of computing in all its aspects, together with a knowledge of fields such as formal logic, psychology, and philosophy — that it is no wonder that CALL has largely remained as it was in the late 1970s. I am sure that in my attempts to encompass the interdisciplinary challenge of AI as it relates to CALL you will detect significant failures on my part, for which I duly apologize in advance. What I have set out to achieve is to make the first faltering step towards establishing the ground for possible advance, as well as alerting the reader to both the difficulties and the real dangers that may lie ahead.

1.6   A VOYAGE OF DISCOVERY

In pursuing this investigation, what follows should be regarded more as a voyage of discovery than as a prescriptive textbook, and it represents the views, experiments and speculations of one who wandered into humanities computing almost by mistake in the 1960s and has never escaped the clutches of the computer since. The book was written in a similar spirit to the account I found in the work of the American writer and critic Bernard DeVoto as to how a certain scientific monograph had come into being:

> A friend of mine, a geneticist, told me he was writing a book and when I flippantly asked why said a true thing: 'In order to find out what I know about genetics'. (DeVoto, 1950, p. 79.)

I am writing these pages in some measure at least in order to find out what, if anything, I know about AI and the extent to which that knowledge can be applied to CALL. As a by-product, I hope that it will also serve the purpose of offering an effective and relatively painless means of enabling the reader to gain a basic knowledge of the main features and potentialities of some of the diversities of AI in relation to the teaching of natural languages without their having to plough through all the vast literature on the subject.

Sifting through the literature on AI has, for reasons which I indicated earlier, itself proved quite a daunting task for a variety of different reasons. As we shall see, many of the problems involved centre round the fact that AI has from the outset faced a series of identity crises. It has never been clear what it really signifies (or whether it is nothing more than a whole range of disparate research endeavours collected for the sake of convenience under one banner). As a result, material relevant to AI is to be found not only in the computing literature, but in that of psychology, philosophy, linguistics, geography, medicine, biology, and many other areas. In addition, it reaches out into fields such as robotics, computer vision, new logics for AI, and many more areas. And it can be more than problematic trying to sort out aspiration from actuality, distinguishing the achievements which have been made from those which are 'just around the corner'.

The reader who is generally unconvinced about the merits of computer-based technology in language teaching may well fear what I have to say represents yet another attempt to take the proverbial sledgehammer to crack the pedagogical nut, to seek to engage the massive resources of an alien technology with a huge expenditure of time and effort (let alone scarce resources) in order to achieve not very much at all. Practical experience has taught us all in the languages field that educational technology can be cumbersome, expensive, unreliable, pedagogically unsound, time-consuming, and in the last analysis at best not cost-effective, and at worst entirely inappropriate.

Although language teachers as a body have been more ready than most to accept and explore the pedagogical potential of new technologies as they have emerged — language laboratory, videocassette, videodisc, direct broadcasting by satellite, and so forth — there has always been a perfectly understandable element of resistance to applying the computer to language teaching at all. The more complex the technology, the greater the input of time and expertise required to achieve an end result, and the more it seems that the learner is being taken away from the one ideal teaching situation, that of the human-to-human interaction of gifted language teacher and committed learner.

1.7   THE OBJECTIONS TO TECHNOLOGY

It is worth pausing for a moment to consider the nature and validity of the objections which have been raised against the application of such methodologies in the transmission of language acquisition skills. They should certainly not be dismissed out of hand as the attitudes of a past generation which cannot or will not contemplate change and advance, since language teachers as a group have readily explored any potentially viable new means of adding to their existing techniques in teaching such an open-ended and hugely complex subject as a modern language.

In my perception, these objections fall into three categories: desirability, quality and appropriateness, and range of applicability.

The first objection manifests itself as a philosophical resistance to seeking to bring together a mindless machine and the infinite complexities and imponderables of natural language. It is by no means a trivial objection founded upon the cultural parochialism of the humanities academic, but sets out from the quite solid premise that the perceived nature of human language is light years away from the perceived current potential of the computer, not least because language is centrally concerned with that most difficult area for computing, that of the interface between the internal processor and the world outside, between the brain and the organs of sight, hearing and speech. Indeed, it is not unreasonable to voice basic doubts about attempting to mechanize processes which we as human beings are a very long way from understanding in any depth ourselves.

On a relatively simple level at least, such fears have, to my satisfaction and to that of many CALL researchers at least, proved groundless, though quite understandable in retrospect. Within a certain restricted subset of language acquisition skills, the computer has been demonstrated to be capable of playing at least a positive remedial role in the classroom. There has been a modest but growing number of respectable research projects which have employed the computer for purposes central to CALL, as well as in other areas of linguistic and literary research.

The second objection is levelled at the real quality of the products of CALL, and particularly of the less than first-rate packages which have found their way into the market place. It is unfortunate that outsiders to CALL in the language field have all too often tended to judge the whole undertaking on the basis of seeing one badly designed piece of software at work, but the objections are not without merit, and are worth examining in some detail. Coupled with this concern is the equally understandable argument that in times like these there is no place for such research work, which is so expensive in terms of time and money, and the results of which are as yet unproven, to say the least.

Here, then, the debate has taken place on the practical rather than on the philosophical plane. The argument goes like this: if this or that piece of software is all that CALL can do and if it does it so badly, then language teachers should not be meddling with computers at all, despite the well-known bandwagon effect which dictates that in order to be in the vanguard of language teaching advances you need at least one computerized language laboratory to show off to the admiring visitors. This 'keeping up with the academic Joneses' may be regarded at first blush as a somewhat trivial observation, but I am firmly of the view that the way in which language-teaching research is funded and the manner in which 'glamorous' hi-tech research gets best funded can actually distort any real advances into this area.

At a time when the resource base is actually shrinking, researchers are naturally led into those areas which are fashionable from the fund-attracting point of view and which are perceived to be capable of generating positive results in the short term, and yet there has been more than one project in the areas of CALL and IV (interactive video) which has promised a great deal, but in which a considerable investment of money and research effort has generated a very modest outcome. The internal pressures on a team whose livelihood depends on the continuation of funding are understandable, but the objective evaluation of results on the part of the unconvinced outsider is likely to have a financially negative impact on all research in the field, whether well-founded or not.

In this respect, it is true that the objectors do have a valid point in relation to the quality of material produced. There is some pretty awful CALL about, some of it quite recent in origin and marketed by very prestigious publishers indeed. The objections, however, are largely misdirected. There is clearly a range of quality in CALL, as there is in any kind of teaching material, but the predominance of less than adequate material can be attributed, not so much to the deficiencies of the medium, but rather to the fact that language teachers have become their own programmers, taken up the computing challenge, and over-hastily went public with the results of their own efforts. Their lack of formal training in computing techniques did not prevent them from making progress of a kind, but it did expose their weaknesses, which were caused by inadequate or partial knowledge of the medium within which they were working.

The final objection is one which I have heard voiced more in university departments than elsewhere, and that is that CALL, if it is admitted to have any value at all, is strictly limited in that value to the relatively early stages of language learning, and therefore has no relevance in the major university language departments, such as those of French and German, where students arrive with a knowledge at least equivalent to Scottish Higher or Advanced Level. Leaving aside the fact that, for a variety of reasons, teaching foreign languages like French and German at university increasingly involves beginners with a wide variety of differing needs and attainment objectives, the work of Farrington in Aberdeen on French prose translation (Farrington, 1981, 1986), and myself and my colleagues Lewis and Johnston in Dundee (Last and Lewis, 1985), together with other projects in Exeter and elsewhere, demonstrates that, although there is a greater challenge in an application of the computer at an advanced level to the teaching of a foreign language, it is one that has been successfully met in those centres and elsewhere.

Indeed, if the distinction between 'teaching language' and teaching in related areas such as literature, politics, history and so forth is disregarded, as it tends to be in most language departments, work such as I have been conducting with students in enhancing their literary and essay-writing skills indicates a very promising role for the computer at an advanced under-graduate level.

In response to all these objections, I would say first that, in common with other researchers, I am emphatically not in favour of 'having a go' at CALL simply because the technology exists and one might as well try it out to see what happens. Nor am I involved in this field because it is currently in vogue. I am convinced that CALL in its present state of development has made a positive, viable and cost-effective contribution within its limitations to the teaching of modern languages (and indeed further to the related subjects that form part of the languages curriculum beyond the beginning stages), and for that reason alone it is well worth considering exploring how that contribution can be extended within the constraints of the current level of generally available microcomputing technology and the considerable body of research work which relates to AI applied to that technology. I fully recognize, though, that the contribution of CALL has by no means been as substantial as it could and might have been, for the reasons which I have enumerated already.

It is all too easy to state that the early enthusiast language teachers cum programmers should have developed their understanding of the computer to a much more advanced level before going into the computing equivalent of print. But the first steps in any new field are inevitably somewhat faltering, and the pioneers have to make them before more polished efforts follow.

Secondly, the research effort of CALL to date has succeeded in providing a sound basis for any potential advance in the future as well as having a considerable spin-off value in making us think through the implications of some of our teaching techniques with more precision.

Taking CALL a stage further will indeed mean moving into much more challenging uncharted territory, but even if it proves ultimately unsuccessful, similar secondary advantages will, I am sure, accrue. The same has already proved to be the case with AI itself. In the same way that it may not have been directly useful and cost-effective to send a man to the moon but the spin-off effect in scientific and other research was substantial indeed — some of this exercized a direct impact on the evolution of the microprocessor itself — the investigation of AI techniques offers many valuable insights into human thought processes and the possibility of constructing computational models of them. That remains true even if the dreamed-of AI revolution never becomes a practical reality.

1.8   A SOUND BASIS FOR TECHNOLOGICAL ADVANCE

CALL, then, has reached something of a plateau, a period of consolidation after the initial outburst of enthusiastic but not always high-quality programming. When programs had matured sufficiently to be placed on public sale (and, as I have hinted, in some cases well before they had reached maturity), it soon became apparent that the harsh facts of the marketplace were also to exert a severely restricting influence on the development of CALL. This pattern of enthusiasm followed by puzzled disenchantment seems to have been shared by many involved in CALL. A typical view is expressed by Duranni in one of the Exeter CALL conference papers:

> All I had at the point of departure was a dim awareness that the computer could be the most powerful tool to have been placed at the disposal of the teaching profession since the invention of the slate. And the more I realized its potential, the more difficult it

became to overlook the fact that it was not being exploited to the full either by educationalists or by the software industry. (Duranni, 1986, p. 27.)

That reference to 'industry' prompts me to record that little has been written about the interrelationship between arts research and the market-place, not least, I suspect, because the existence of any such interaction would be flatly denied by the academic engaged in 'pure research' which is of no commercial value, but which has (so it is hoped) a considerable, if unquantifiable, impact within the relatively narrow confines of a particular specialism.

But even the researcher into Renaissance literature or eighteenth-century dialect poetry, if he wants to see that research in print, is obliged at some stage to come into contact, however indirectly, with non-academics who function in the real world of investment and return, profit and loss. This book, for example, would never have seen the light of day had Ellis Horwood not considered that it was a viable financial proposition as well as not entirely lacking in academic merit.

Such an interaction between academia and Mammon, however unwilling humanities academics may be to admit its existence, has actually played a very substantial role indeed in the short history of CALL and in my estimation contributes substantially to the explanation as to why CALL has now reached a developmental impasse. I indicated earlier that there were, so to speak, internal reasons why CALL had not advanced. These related, you will recall, largely to the steepness of the learning curve for those seeking to master the research literature of AI and the expenditure of time and effort involved. But there are external reasons, too, and largely commercial ones at that.

This is not the first time that educational technology has been impeded by market forces in the arts disciplines. The language laboratory was seen as a great advance in language-teaching methodologies, but the shiny new equipment did not attract sufficient courseware in either quantity or quality for it even to approach the realization of its potential in real terms, not least because it was not regarded as a commercially viable proposition. Now, ironically, the language laboratory has simultaneously slipped from favour and at the same time promises to take a major leap forward in the form of the interactive computerized laboratory.

The difficulties confronting IV are equally substantial, despite the promise which the technology holds out. Recouping the cost of investment into the design and mastering of laserdiscs (which runs into tens of thousands of pounds) is not likely to be a feasible proposition in private-sector financial terms, and the severe constraints on research funding in colleges and universities render it unlikely that videodisc technology will have the impact which it deserves. However, this may not in time turn out to be the missed opportunity that it seems to be, because the advent of CD-ROM and interactive CD (CDI) technology with its broad consumer base and the potential for the user to master his own material (using the quaintly titled WORM — write once, read many times — technology) may well not only replace the videodisc but far outstrip its potentiality. Already it is possible to mix audio and visual signals on compact disc.

A secure position in the retail marketplace is a humdrum but unavoidable prerequisite for a successful piece of technological hardware in the educational market. As a former consultant to a company which produced, amongst other equipment, computer-controlled language laboratories and recorders, I gained an insight into the difficulties of a commercial company devising a pricing structure which would maximize the market penetration of their equipment whilst still enabling them to recoup the considerable sums spent on research and development of equipment, much of which was so specialized that it had no wider applicability than the limited — and fairly crowded — marketplace of modern languages teaching, where the purchasing power of individual departments or local authorities was not of a very high order.

For commercial reasons alone, the chances are that, as I suggested just now, the compact-disc player as a storage device or interactive system, or its variants in WORM or read–write technology will have a much greater impact as a repository of huge databases, visual, audio, and in the form of computer files and programs. With a sufficient base in the mass consumer market, the product availability and future development will be secure enough for specialized versions of that equipment to make its way into the language-teaching field.

In one sense, a consideration of the role of AI in CALL is itself currently being blurred by the arrival of these new technologies which are impacting on CALL from other directions, notably the computer-controlled cassette recorder, speech synthesis, and the CD-ROM, which we have just briefly considered. All these extend the nature of the interaction beyond that of keyboard and silent screen, and raise further issues about the potential of new modalities of interaction in both 'dumb' and 'AI' contexts. But in each case, the market shakedown has yet to be completed and the winners and losers announced. I need hardly remind language teachers of the problems caused by the coexistence of a number of different videocassette standards — the old Philips system, the Philips 2000, Beta, VHS, and others — and the difficulty of transfer between them, let alone the complexities of SECAM, PAL in its various manifestations, NTSC, and new standards which are currently waiting in the wings.

And now the name of the game is being further radically transformed by the development of the concept of hypertext and hypermedia. The notion of the computer-based interactive multimedia non-sequential database threatens to take the educational computing world by storm, although it too is beginning to show signs of the same kind of teething troubles which beset (and continue to plague) AI. The implications of hypertext and hypermedia will be explored later in these pages.

Before I turn to a consideration of the chequered history of CALL and AI to date, however, there are two preliminary matters to be resolved, both of which I have already indicated are of central importance. The first is that of expertise, the second relates to theory.

1.9   THE QUESTION OF EXPERTISE

Although I have written programs in languages as diverse as SNOBOL, FORTH, various assemblers and numerous dialects of BASIC, I am not by training a computer programmer. Nor am I a philosopher, linguistician or psychologist. Those are the four areas of expertise which have tended to claim exclusive rights over AI. Over the years, however, I have consistently argued that the key qualification for anyone designing and implementing a CAL package of any kind is that he or she should be an expert in the subject which is being taught in that package. This has been my considered view since I first became involved in literary programming:

> The scholar who seeks to push back the frontier of knowledge of what the computer can do for him is in something of a quandary. Somehow he must retain his identity as a literary scholar, and yet at the same time contrive to make progress in this new and strange field. This cannot be done by remaining piously aloof from the Computer Centre and by persuading someone else to write the programs for you. Apart from the fact that computer programmers have more than enough work already, mutual misunderstandings can readily arise, as a result of the literary scholar's ignorance of the workings of the machine, and the programmer's ignorance of the techniques of the critic. The only answer is that a new breed of scholars must emerge: the literary programmer. (Last, 1970, p. 483.)

Such a view was quite contentious in the days in which the computer programmer and systems analyst, so to speak, held the keys to the computer room, and the humble user was only allowed access at one remove through his pack of punched cards in batch mode.

Since that time, however, and particularly since the revolution in computing hardware and software wrought by the microcomputer, attitudes have shifted substantially. It is becoming more and more accepted that scholars in all kinds of disciplines, from medicine, physics, and geography even to modern languages, can independently make substantial and powerful use of computing facilities for the furtherance of research and teaching in their subject areas. In one sense, it has become almost too easy to gain instant access to computing power and programming languages and, as was the case with many early CALL programmers, work was done with the barest minimum of knowledge of the implications of the environment within which they were operating.

I detect, however, a resurgence of the 'Keep off the grass' attitude of the early days of computing among certain workers in the field of AI. The feeling is once again abroad in some quarters that unless you have a certain predetermined collection of qualifications you really ought to keep well away from a field which is too conceptually difficult for you to cope with if you lack those qualifications. My view is entirely the opposite. If the computer is a hardware tool which may assist in certain areas of my teaching and research, the concepts of AI, hazy, disparate and incomplete though they may be at their current stage of development, should equally be an accessible intellectual tool at the disposal of scholars in any field. Having made that claim, I must stress that this does not absolve the language teacher cum programmer from acquiring a sufficient level of knowledge and skill before embarking on a career as a CALL programmer.

1.10 A THEORETICAL BASIS

Having considered the question of expertise, I turn now to my second preliminary point, which concerns theory. What follows in this book may be regarded as excessively theoretical and at times rather remote from the practical concerns of CALL.

In reply, I would argue that CALL has to date not been theoretical enough (and that this is precisely why so much of the software on offer is so awful). In the early days of CALL, it was not unacceptable to read that a paper intends to take 'a very practical approach', and that 'in the present state of the art, a computer can best ... reinforce or tell but not teach' (Benwell, 1986), but to find that those words were written in the mid-1980s indicates hardly any advance at all over what the early pioneers of CALL were describing a decade ago and is a depressing reflection on the lack of theoretical underpinning in this field. What passes for theory has too often been merely speculation and assertion, a weakness not restricted to CALL practitioners, as it appears from this psychologist's lament:

> Just pretending that one has a theory of how one process is to access another, by drawing in an arrow between two boxes, butters no parsnips at all. (Allport, 1980, p. 52.)

That is a specific issue to which we shall return when considering the way in which the internal processes of the human mind can be modelled in a computing environment. In a sense, language teachers are in some measure responsible for this lack of a theoretical superstructure to their subject; research in plenty there has been, of course, but the majority of language teachers — those whose research interests do not lie in teaching methodo-logy — tend, I suspect, to be suspicious of change and of the respectability of the theories underpinning the demands for such change. Whilst they publicly acquiesce in innovation, many privately wonder whether this or that breakthrough in language teaching is not so much a genuine step forward, but rather a sideways move around the problem, attacking the same intractable issues from a different direction. While some may feel uncomfortable that there is no universally agreed theoretical underpinning to the language-teaching process, unlike their scientific colleagues with their 'scientific method' of hypothesis building and practical testing, most are content to muddle along without any great awareness of the theory underlying the practice, and without any conviction that if that theory either existed or could be expatiated *in extenso*, it would change their teaching practices one jot.

One crucial reason why CALL is stuck at its present level, economic considerations apart, is that it never really broke away from its image of an area for enthusiastic computing amateurs functioning without a sound basis in theory: 'Theorising is precarious, but if we want to get anywhere, we have to theorise'. (Schlesinger, 1982, p. 76.)

Language teachers have seen all too often in the past the damage that can be wrought by the theoretician insisting that this or that methodology is the one and only true path to language teaching. Instances of this abound, and I actually experienced the rigours of one such orthodoxy when I was a school teacher in the early 1960s, and the school decided to adopt the extremely doctrinaire and 'new-technology' approach of the French CREDIF audio-visual system. The new technology was that of the reel-to-reel recorder and the slide projector. Its worst aspect was the removal of all initiative from the teacher. A certain pattern had to be followed regardless of the actual perceived needs of the learner at a given moment. So I am not surprised that language teachers should be suspicious of theory, and in particular of those who advance a new theory as the sole viable approach to language teaching.

But it is important to differentiate between extremist approaches to language teaching — such as the direct method at one end of the spectrum and prescriptive grammar drilling at the other — which claim the exclusive right as the sole valid approach to the inculcation of language skills, on the one hand, and a sound basis in the generally applicable fundamentals of CALL on the other. Such fundamentals are, if you like, the eternal verities of CALL, which remain valid whatever your confessional affiliations to this or that school of language-teaching thought. And it is a matter of considerable regret that they have not been granted the weight of significance they deserve by the CALL enthusiasts. There is even a shortage of practical guidelines on such straightforward issues as the nature of the user interface. The best statement of good practice in this context is to be found in Davies's excellent introduction to CALL (Davies, 1985).

1.11   A NOTE OF CONTROVERSY

Finally, I had not intended when I first set out to write this book to be so controversial, if that is the right word, both in relation to AI and to the present state of CALL. I feel that it would be dishonest not to have stated at the outset that I approached this project with considerable enthusiasm, which became progressively dampened both by the substantial gap between the promise of AI and the 'media hype' practised within the scientific community as well as in the public media at large, and, more sadly, by the fact that much of the CALL material on general public sale now is in many respects no better than the very first attempts at bringing language teaching and the computer together in the mid-1970s. At least the pioneers then had the excuse that they were breaking new ground. That can hardly be argued now with any credibility.

1.12   THE BOOK IN OVERVIEW

The chapters that follow consider the past, present state and future potentiality of AI in CALL, and I have divided the concepts up as follows. The next chapter considers the 'story so far': the way in which CALL has evolved to its present level of reasonable maturity, without showing any signs of promise that it has a clear future path mapped out for it. Chapter 3 considers the whole question of the nature of AI, and the way in which it can be perceived as a potential route forward for CALL.

In the fourth chapter, the key question of the relationship between learner and machine is considered, since if this is not clearly understood and properly established, then there is little purpose in going forward at all.

The rest of the book considers the problems facing any researcher seeking to advance into AI. First, in Chapter 5, we consider the starting point for CALL moving in the direction of AI. In Chapter 6, we consider the crucial issue of how we can attempt to model the mind of the learner and the learning process. In Chapter 7, we see how expert systems might be applied to this task. Chapter 8 explores possible practical applications of AI in CALL, based on the matters considered in earlier chapters. In a concluding chapter added at a relatively late stage, I consider further new techniques which threaten to alter radically the map of AI and to give the whole field a new impetus and a new direction.

2

The story so far

2.1 INTRODUCTION

In this chapter, we consider in greater depth the issues raised in Chapter 1 relating to the early successes and failures of humanities computing and their implications for CALL, the current state of CALL and the best current practices.

Before posing the question as to how CALL arrived at its present stage of development and whether or not it is prudent to push it forward in the direction of AI, we shall need to spell out the ground rules on which proper practice in CALL should be founded, not least since they appear not to be sufficiently well-known among many CALL practitioners, and we need also to consider how CALL came about and how it has evolved to its present state of development.

2.2 LITERARY AND LINGUISTIC COMPUTING

To step a little out of chronological order, I consider first the developments which took place largely in the UK (although there were scholars active too in the USA, Italy, and elsewhere), and which led to the founding of the ALLC in 1970. I then turn to a brief consideration of mechanical or machine translation (MT) in its first flowering.

This was in the days before on-line multi-user interaction was available, and it might be argued that such developments are irrelevant to an evaluation of CALL. Quite the contrary: what clearly emerged from the work of the early researchers into literary and linguistic computing set the agenda and established the parameters for the initial phase of CALL. The successes and failures of the first literary computing experts, together with the less than happy results of early MT work, pointed the directions in which CALL could most successfully function and, equally importantly, which areas should, for the present at least, be avoided.

One of the founders of the ALLC, R. A. Wisbey, is a German medievalist scholar. Curiously, perhaps, many of the computing pioneers in language and literature are Germanists, and many of them medievalists at that. There are two main reasons why this is the case, neither of which have any connection with the supposed logicality of the agglutinative, inflected structure of the German language, nor with the supposed characteristics of the German nation and its literature.

The first reason is that, being a minority language (in the number of staff and students involved, I hasten to add, not in its significance), there has always been both more pressure to employ techniques suitable for *ab initio* learners who lack the leisure of four or five years' study, as in French, before reaching Ordinary Level or its equivalent and more pressure on limited staff to deploy their skills as effectively and widely as possible.

In addition, there is no doubt that, for the English speaker, German is a more demanding language to master, especially when it is taught as a second foreign language after French, and the learners' expectations are geared to the levels of difficulty experienced in that language, and that more rigorous techniques are required to ensure that the learner has properly assimilated all the simultaneous challenges presented by exercising productive skills in German: word endings, cases, word order, and so forth.

In that respect, the evolution of CALL — or rather, the potential for it to emerge when the technology produced an appropriate modality of interaction — was very much demand-led, if you like, and in retrospect it seems almost inevitable that Germanists led the way, followed rapidly by Hispanists and others in minority languages.

On the other side of the coin, the medievalist's involvement was not particularly due so much to any specifically Germanist approach, except that German literary scholarship was singularly deficient in the kind of aids like concordances and word indexes that abounded in English and in the classics. The impetus came from the pioneering spirit of Wisbey, who saw the potential even in the early days of computing at Cambridge university, and managed to persuade that traditional collegiate institution to establish under his leadership the LLCC (Literary and Linguistic Computing Centre).

In one of the key papers of early literary computing, Wisbey records how the most successful early applications of the computer to the humanities, and in particular the study of medieval German language and literature, involved a more or less straightforward computerization of a mechanical process — the compilation of a word index or concordance — which had in the past demanded an almost impossible combination of editorial skill and infinite patience in a task of extreme tedium. In these labours of love which consumed decades of a scholar's lifetime,

> certain patterns are unmistakable. The mature scholar tells of how, misled by inexperience and youthful enthusiasm he rashly embarked upon the task which has accompanied him through two, three, or even four decades. (Wisbey, 1962, p. 160.)

Following in the footsteps of R. Busa, the first scholar to employ punched-card and later computing equipment in a major concordance project (an *Index Thomisticus*, to the complete works of St Thomas Aquinas), Wisbey employed computing techniques in the creation of concordances to medieval German texts. Curiously, although English literature was in the precomputer days already very well served by concordances to the major writers, German literary texts had been seriously neglected, and even Goethe had been almost completely ignored in this regard. For his first project, Wisbey selected a text known as the *Wiener Genesis*, all 28 000 words of which were punched on to paper tape (the input medium for the EDSAC 2 computer then in use), which presented technical difficulties, since the five-hole tape coped only with upper case characters, digits, and mathematical symbols. The first phase of the project was to produce an index only. The ultimate intention was to produce a concordance.

Even given the slowness of the peripheral equipment (punched-tape machines and teleprinter output) and the novel nature of the programming required, it was clear that the automation of the concordance process released the scholar to concentrate on the more intellectually demanding aspects of the undertaking, such as dealing with homonyms and lemmatization.

This undertaking demonstrated, then, that in the context of a clearly quantifiable exercise the computer had an immense potential not only to remove the 'mindless and stultifying drudgery' (Wisbey, 1962) of compiling such material but also to advance the work of the scholar. This, of course, took the form of enabling him to concentrate on what the human scholar was best suited for, which points the way to the most successful distribution of labour in this field between scholar and computer. But another aspect of the involvement of the computer also rapidly became evident.

Once the text of the work or corpus to be concorded or index had been painstakingly written out on index cards in the precomputing days and had been sorted into alphabetical order, not only did the entire text have to be set in type, which involves — as a swift calculation will determine — typing out the equivalent of the entire work of an author several times over, with all the implications for error that such a procedure invites, but also the entire pack of index cards instantly becomes so much waste paper, with no further value in the project.

The computerization of concordances transformed this situation by requiring the text to be keyed in once only, and as I discovered in my own early work in this field, long before the days of word processors with spelling checkers, one of the best ways of discovering the major classes of typographical errors in a text was to sort it into alphabetical order and to examine closely all the words which occurred only once. Then the correction could be made on the punched cards or tape and the process of concording repeated.

But even more importantly, it soon occurred to workers like Wisbey that, once the text had been used for an alphabetical sort, it remained available in its original form for any number of other quantifiable processes, such as a reverse index, which, not least in Middle High German, has very great value in determining the role and nature of suffixes in the text. In fact, as Wisbey recognized, the original input text has huge potential:

> The really exciting vistas however, begin to open up when one
> considers that once texts have been put on tape they constitute a

permanent archive for linguistic research.... Word counts and statistics of many different kinds can also be readily obtained. (Wisbey, 1962, p. 172.)

The LLCC led more or less directly to the foundation of the ALLC in 1972 after a first conference on literary and linguistic computing in Cambridge, which was attended by pioneers from around the world. An additional impetus came about by the enthusiastic efforts of a staff member of the Regional Computing Centre in the University of Manchester, Joan Smith, who swiftly recognized that a small but dedicated band of enthusiasts were turning to the computer as a means of resolving quantitative issues in literary and linguistic computing, and founded a newsletter, from which the ALLC and its publications evolved and grew.

So it was that one strand of humanities computing evolved from using the computer as a high-speed clerical worker, as a compiler of concordances, reverse indexes and the like at one end of the scale, to highly complex interactive analyses of textual patterns, and into areas such as disputed authorship and automatic parsing at the other.

In this regard, the successes recorded were almost in direct proportion to the extent to which the task being computerized was straightforwardly clerical in nature. In other words, concordances, word counts, reverse indexes and the like opened up whole new areas of opportunities for scholars to investigate text, whether from a literary or linguistic point of view — or indeed, from a combination of both, for one of the great positive benefits of the computer's involvement in the humanities (and, I suspect, the sciences, too) is that it has assisted in breaking down the artificial barriers that have existed both within individual disciplines and between subject areas, not just within the humanities but beyond to the sciences.

However, the more the emphasis shifted from 'quantity' to 'quality', as it were, the more problematical the investigations became, and the greater the awareness grew in areas such as the statistical study of text that we were not dealing with a phenomenon of the order of, say, rainfall statistics, where first the total amount of rainfall was known, and the impact of that rainfall was more or less linearly related to the amount of precipitation.

In other words, if Shakespeare uses so many words in a play, we do not know the total population of words which he had, either actively, or passively, at his disposal. Nor are words simple building bricks in the total impact of the text: nouns can be referred to by pronouns or by ellipsis, and a simple head count will not elicit a straightforward graphic relationship with their significance. In fact, a word used once — or even, not at all — can dominate an entirely literary work.

Further than that, scholars were beginning to realize that the 'boring' little words which take up to half of a text (words like 'the', 'and', 'but', 'or', and so forth) are not to be discarded as uninteresting or unyielding of positive results. They can be valid indicators of subconscious stylistic patterns and thought structures within the text.

Such concepts were taken up and exploited in disputed authorship studies, an area fraught with controversy and complexities. Here statistics were being applied to prove or disprove authorship of documents or literary texts, and it was clear that such investigations on the computer — trying to use the machine to prove who wrote Shakespeare, if you like — were not the straightforward extrapolation of the purely quantitative studies that many had in their early enthusiasms thought they would be.

The more, then, that research moved from fixed quantities (which may then be subjected to qualitative evaluation away from the computer), the greater the difficulties became, and it was evident that in many areas at least those difficulties were to prove insuperable.

2.3   MECHANICAL TRANSLATION (MT)

The second of the two strands which preceded the invention of CALL derived from what has, rightly or wrongly, been regarded as the first halting steps in the direction of AI, in the shape of the abortive early attempts at MT. Unlike literary and linguistic computing, however, the main thrust of MT took place in the USA, where sufficient funding was available for the substantial investment required to explore its potential.

MT as conceived in its early days was founded on false premises, not so much because of the inadequacy of contemporary computing equipment to cope with the processing required within a manageable time scale, but because it was founded on erroneous assumptions about the nature of human language. The whole undertaking was regarded as essentially little more than an extension of the considerable cryptographic effort undertaken during the Second World War, to an increasing extent on a mechanized basis. The much-quoted memorandum circulated in 1949 by Warren Weaver, sometime vice-president of the Rockefeller foundation, poses the question as to whether 'the problem of translation could conceivably be treated as a problem in cryptography'. It is all too easy now to look back with the clarity of hindsight and point to the glaring deficiencies in such a line of argumentation.

After an over-enthusiastic beginning, which was fuelled by the explosion in scientific publications in major languages other than English, notably Russian, optimism that fully automated translation was just around the corner began to wane, and large question marks were placed in America over the huge amounts of money invested in MT projects. A committee of the National Academy of Sciences, formed ad hoc and called the Automatic Language Processing Advisory Committee (more widely known under its acronym of ALPAC), reported in 1966 that the millions of dollars invested in MT research had yielded a paltry harvest.

This phenomenon of initial success being held in restraint by what appear to be secondary problems but which turn out to be insuperable stumbling blocks is one which we shall find again and again in AI research: 'The history of MT has numerous examples of methods which promised much at first but proved disappointing failures' (Hutchins, 1986, p. 328). The temptation to construct a small-scale project with clear limitations, pronounce the results successful, and then attempt to scale that project up, is considerable, but it is precisely when the attempt is made to expand a modest experiment into full-blooded MT that difficulties multiply. The reason is that it is not just a matter of scaling up, but of extending the project into quite different areas with many more complex and not readily quantifiable parameters. It is an almost classic syndrome for such investigations, and the reasons underlying the pattern are ones we shall have to explore if the same mistakes are not to be made in AI-based CALL.

It was clear, then, that although there were certain areas in which the computer functioned well, there were other, crucial phases, notably that of synthesis (generating appropriate output in the target language) in which it failed to produce quality results. Indeed, as far back as 1959, Yehoshua Bar-Hillel, one of the best-known researchers in the field, wrote a report in very negative terms indeed, as described by Hutchins:

> The basic argument was that MT research was, with few exceptions, mistakenly pursuing an unattainable goal: fully automatic translation of a quality equal to that of a good human translator. Instead, it should be less ambitious and work towards the realisation of systems involving human collaboration. (Hutchins, 1986, p. 154.)

Once the lifeblood of financial support had more or less dried up, it seemed that MT was doomed to disappear from the academic agenda of AI. There are fashions in all areas of academic research, and MT rapidly lost its charismatic appeal as the linguistic equivalent of transplant surgery and entered a long period of quiescence. Recently, however, there has been a resurgence of interest in the field, largely for two reasons.

On the one hand, computing equipment has become so much more powerful and immeasurably cheaper now than it was in the days when MT was first mooted. Indeed, there is clear evidence that many of the intractable problems of the first phase can be overcome by 'brute-force' programming and huge databases, and, although this is in many respects simply a matter of moving the goalposts and creating a new, and even more intractable set of problems at the outer limits of AI advance, there is an interesting but rarely expressed notion of intelligence to be found lurking among the vast amounts of computing power coming on to our desktops and into our computing laboratories. With the introduction of Risc chips, parallel processors and gigabytes of almost instant-access storage, I detect an argument emerging which we shall have to consider later: namely, that if computing power, speed and architecture continue to advance at their present rate (possibly into optical or even bio-computers), then the 'brick wall' which we inevitably run up against in AI work will be pushed so far back by raw computing power that we can generate systems which act intelligently even though they have no innate 'intelligence'.

On the other hand, there have been strong commercial pressures in an age of expensive translating manpower and the increasing internationalization of trade for the creation of computerized aids to translation, from glorified electronic dictionaries at one end of the scale to far more ambitious projects at the other.

Among the commercially available MT products, the ALPS system is more of an electronic assistant to the translator than an MT system in its own right, although there is no doubt that on-line dictionary support such as ALPS offers constitutes a substantial supportive environment for the human translator to operate in. The Weidner package is more ambitious in that it offers a rough and ready translation for the human post-editor to polish into a more fluent and natural format. For a discussion of these and other projects, see Hutchins (1986, pp. 293ff) and Lewis (1985).

In the world of trade and commerce, the European Common Market represents a sufficiently strong user base for translation among its member-country languages (and the potential number of language pairs is frighteningly high) for a new high-priority, and high-cost, project to be undertaken. Substantial sums are being invested into the Eurotra MT project, which is the most ambitious MT venture ever undertaken, and which holds out the promise of a much higher level of success in automatic translation. But as Lewis points out in his recent overview of the history of MT:

> MT is, however, certainly here to stay and has become 'of age' and, as a tool for human use, may well be considered to possess neither more nor fewer limitations than computer assisted language learning programs and packages in the current state of the art. (Lewis, 1985, p. 50.)

Although Lewis overstates somewhat the gulf between aspiration and actuality in the two different spheres, the parallels are too close for comfort. The reasons, though, are quite different. Whereas MT aimed too high, most of CALL has never even begun to aim high enough.

2.4   THE DEVELOPMENT OF CALL

CALL played no part in the early days of humanities computing. The first real work began when on-line interaction became a practical reality. My own early experiments on the mainframe computing system at Hull University served both to demonstrate that CALL (although in those days it had yet to be baptized as such) was indeed a practical possibility, but the mainframe environment with its uncertain response times and user interface designed for professional programmers rather than first-time users underlined the fact that it was an idea whose time had really yet to come. It was in the field of undergraduate teaching of quantitative techniques in literary analysis that the computer appeared at that stage of its development to find its proper role in humanities teaching.

As well as supervising PhD students who employed concordances and quantitative techniques in their literary research, I conducted a series of Honours Options classes in computational stylistics, based on programs which enabled the text under investigation to be processed both off-line (in the form of concordances, word frequency listings, and the like), and interactively, with students searching for specific strings of characters within the text and evaluating their significance. Here, as might have been expected, the real interest centres on the borderline between quantity and quality. Despite the technical difficulties it presented, it at least permitted genuinely innovative investigation in a new field by students at an undergraduate level.

Much later in this book, we shall be encountering hypertext and the concept of 'navigating' through a large database of very complex structure. It was precisely this notion which, although not ennobled with that title, made the on-line string-searching facility, for example, such an exciting tool to work with. As well as searching for known features of the text, it readily enabled new textual features to be discovered, even by searching the text for the occurrences of the copula or commas, or even clusters of letters within words. For an example of how that serendipitous on-line investigation can throw up fascinating results, see Last and Lewis (1985).

Of the validity of such work, at both undergraduate and research level, there can be no doubt, so long, that is, as the limitations of the techniques involved are fully recognized. The computer has made its strong and growing impact in the humanities not because it was a shiny new technological toy which just had to be taken out of the cupboard to be played with; its substantial presence now in the humanities is due entirely to the fact that it has proven itself an invaluable tool, even at the level of the humble word-processor, which has transformed the productivity and work style of countless humanities academics. The growth of the ALLC bears eloquent testimony to the rich opportunities for computer applications in both literary and linguistic research, once the basic principles are clearly understood (see the journal *Literary and Linguistic Computing*). Such work could — and, until recently, it could be argued, must — be conducted in a mainframe environment, but with CALL this was clearly not the case.

The real prerequisite for the first full flowering of CALL was a computing environment which was not hostile to the casual user of applications programs; which supported rather than deterred interactive terminal sessions; and which permitted the use of foreign character sets and full-screen addressing, and possessed a moderate graphics capability.

That potentiality was only released when the microcomputer in its various manifestations became generally available.

2.5 THE ADVENT OF THE MICRO

The development of CALL in the UK (which has been the dominant centre for this research activity) was crucially affected by the production of one particular microcomputer, the BBC Micro, whose market penetration in a wide range of departments in schools and colleges has been so considerable that it provided almost the sole logical target machine for the development and publication of software which enabled CALL to take the first important step forward but which has also contributed significantly to the present static state of the art.

As I have argued elsewhere, the great government initiative to place a micro in every secondary school (maths cupboard, usually), was far from being the brave new innovative venture which it was claimed to be. This has turned out to be the case not only because one micro in a school of well over a thousand pupils is a pitifully inadequate allocation, almost worse than useless, but also because no one seemed to have thought out why, precisely, the micro was being introduced in the first place (to teach computing, perhaps, or for quite different purposes).

The dominance of the BBC micro, although introducing the elements of CALL to many people, has had a negative impact on the development of CALL. It has led a whole generation of learners (and, even worse, teachers and program designers) into a computing dead end. Whilst the 'real world' of computing was moving increasingly in the direction of the MSDOS and Unix operating systems, and using machines of substantially more power and RAM than the BBC B with its meagre 32K allocation, the stranglehold of the BBC micro increased, not least in the language-teaching environment. In addition, the BBC micro turned out to be increasingly the expensive option, and one of a growing tangle of upgrades and add-ons, causing problems of compatibility in a system which should at least have had the merit of uniformity of application across the range — or, at least, upwards compatibility.

Teachers new to computing not unnaturally tended to assume that what the BBC micro had to offer somehow represented a computing 'norm', and, once they had invested a considerable amount of time and effort into finding their way about its splendid dialect of BASIC and thoroughly well integrated operating system, they have turned out to be not surprisingly reluctant to saddle themselves with all the attendant problems of learning all over again about new and unfamiliar systems.

It is a significant but not often fully enough recognized fact that there is a considerable amount of inertia built into the human side of the computing environment. People who are busy enough in their mainstream activities are reluctant in the extreme to surrender their expertise, as it were, and become beginners all over again on a new operating system or a new computer language. And on the software side, huge investment of time and effort in 'ancient' languages such as COBOL and FORTRAN and the packages which have been written in those languages present an almost irresistible conservative pull on the penetration of new languages, new operating environments, and new hardware advances.

There has been a curious spin-off effect of this phenomenon in the number of BBC BASIC emulators available on the IBM PC range, and even on machines like the Amiga 500 and 2000. This may seem to offer a software upgrade path, but it is not without problems, not least if you are a mixed-language programmer (BASIC and 6502 assembler) or make heavy use of the *FX and VDU commands. The problems of portability, though, are clearly being faced in order to meet the resistance of those wedded to a particular system, and the increasing use of languages like C for the design of software is also making life easier for the CALL programmer, but only on systems with a generous availability of RAM.

CALL started off with a considerable disadvantage, then, in the hardware and software environment in which it was constrained, for the most part, to operate. But this was compounded by the fact that the programming of CALL material was being carried out, as I indicated earlier, almost exclusively by language teachers who were, not unnaturally, thoroughly conversant with their discipline and enthusiastic to a fault to experiment with this exciting new medium. At the same time, however, few had any real background in proper computing practice, nor indeed, in crucial issues like the nature of the human–computer interface (which we shall be examining in some depth in Chapter 4).

As a result, the deficiencies of early CALL material were all too evident: it is true to say that CALL started off with considerable built-in handicaps for the reasons which I have just outlined. But it is equally true that CALL practitioners should have learned from their early mistakes and advanced the quality and maturity of their material. All too often, as we shall see, this is far from having been the case. CALL may have started from behind, but it has had the best part of a decade to catch up, and do more besides.

There is one unfortunate side-effect of the early CALL programs which merits a moment's consideration, and that is the fact that their simplicity in design seemed to indicate that the programmer/teachers of those days were wedded to the behaviourist view of language teaching. It is important that the record should be set straight in this regard. Linear programs — that is, programs which took the learner from beginning to end with no built-in options or branches within them — were regarded by some as symptomatic of this approach to the learner and the learning situation.

I was not a little amused to find my own early mainframe CALL work on the receiving end of strictures from a leading figure in the CALL field:

> Last ... describes a program to teach German which is strictly Skinnerian (apart from a generous concession to allow two tries at each question). (O'Shea and Self, 1983, p. 71.)

I must confess that, on reading those words, I felt rather like the character in the Molière play who discovered to his surprise that he had been speaking in prose when all along he had thought that he was spouting alexandrines. I must further confess my ignorance, since I had at that time not the faintest idea of who Skinner was and what dreadful theories he had enunciated. The writers of CALL programs in the early days were simply trying to come to terms with a new technology and exploit it as best they could. As it happened, it was possible to put together tutorial question and answer programs with a fairly limited knowledge of programming. As to the learning techniques involved, it was some time before the recognition gained currency that there were a whole series of different kinds of skills to be acquired by the teacher anxious to exploit computing technology in the most effective and appropriate manner.

Still, there are always academics who are more concerned with theory in the wrong sense, rather than with practice. In fact, my programs were 'branching' in the very simpleminded sense that students were encouraged to try out back-up exercises if they did not perform well, and, more importantly, to 'branch' away from the computer altogether in the direction of my office for a personal discussion of linguistic difficulties. Inadequate the programming methodology of the CALL pioneers may have been, doctrinaire it most emphatically was not.

Two factors inhibit CALL at this point in time from making the kind of advances which are necessary to move it away from the first generation of such software. The first is the lack of a generally agreed set of criteria for the present generation of CALL. Whether or not such criteria have broad approval in theory, it is sadly clear from the generality of CALL practice, even now after more than a decade of existence, that a very great deal is left to be desired.

The second, and by far the more substantial, is the steepness of the learning curve which faces those involved in CALL who wish to move in the direction of AI-like programs and software. In the early days, anyone with sufficient enthusiasm, a smattering of BASIC, and the brass neck to demonstrate pretty inadequate programs in public could count themselves as CALL programmers. But now the initial pioneering days are over, and a great deal of material has to be mastered by anyone seeking to acquire expertise in this field. Nowhere is this more true than in the case of AI applications.

2.6 THE NEGATIVE IMPACT OF THE LANGUAGE LABORATORY

Language teachers have as a body always demonstrated a commendably practical and pragmatic approach to new technology, being ever anxious to explore unfamiliar territory in the cause of transmitting language skills to a group of learners. This positive attitude towards technological innovation was, however, somewhat dented by the arrival in the 1950s of the language laboratory, which failed to measure up to its promise of revolutionizing language teaching and which, in its earlier reel-to-reel manifestations, tended to be less than reliable. It was also perceived as being wedded to one particular approach to language teaching, that of the behaviourist school.

Appropriate courseware for the laboratory was conspicuous by its absence, and much of what did appear tended regrettably to mould itself to fit the limitations of the technology rather than to reflect the best teaching practice, especially at a time when the behaviourist approach to language teaching was under serious challenge. In addition, the terminology — language laboratory — was itself unfortunate, lending an unwelcome pseudoscientific aura to language teaching in that context. On top of that, the logistics of ensuring that learners appeared at the right time, listening to the correct tapes on equipment that actually worked properly, militated against the open-armed acceptance of this cumbersome and expensive educational tool.

The language laboratory also made language teachers realize that educational technology is costly, and not just in money terms: the amount of time and effort required to put a small programme onto tape caused considerable questioning as to the cost-effectiveness of the laboratory as a teaching medium.

A further potential demerit of the language laboratory lay in the fact that it offered a less than stimulating environment for the learner, threatening at best tedium, at worst serious sensory deprivation. Sitting in a little box staring at a blank wall and listening to a poor-quality tape recording of a foreign national and then reproducing the desired response (with no instant feedback, unless the teacher happened to be monitoring the right booth at the crucial moment) was not exactly designed to foster committed learning of a foreign language. True, many attempts have been made since the early days to improve all aspects of the language laboratory, but the concerns among the language teaching profession which it generated were, not surprisingly, transferred to the computer when CALL came on the scene.

Once again, it appeared that alien technology was being forced into service, teaching the wrong skills in the wrong way on unreliable and unfriendly equipment. Besides, it was argued by some, the use to which the computer was being put was at a very low level indeed: the full potential of the technology was far from being exploited, and it was simply a waste of time and effort to underuse such an expensive resource. Another educational technology toy was, it seemed, once more being recruited at considerable expense of time and effort in order to achieve hardly anything at all. The same argument is being put forward by a substantial proportion of those who have acquired DBS (direct broadcasting by satellite) systems.

I leave on one side the much-employed but to me quite illogical argument that the computer is somehow being 'underused' in some aspects of CALL. I can see the argument in the case of thousands of pounds' worth of equipment being used as a hand calculator, but that is a fairly extreme case. If the computer is performing a task which cannot readily be undertaken on other equipment, then it is not being underused, even though, as say in the case of word processing (arguably the commonest use of microcomputing equipment), it could be argued that the microprocessor spends most of its time sitting around waiting between keystrokes. But, then, one wonders how the computing purists would have those valuable nanoseconds employed. The real issue here is not supposed underuse, but inappropriate use of the computer (or any other form of educational technology from chalkboard to videodisc).

However, instead of dreaming the impossible dream of what the ideal intelligent computer tutoring system might offer at some remote future date, small bands of enthusiasts mastered the much-maligned language BASIC on their microcomputers (to wildly varying levels of competence) and began to explore the possibilities of computer applications in language teaching in the face of considerable scepticism, if not outright hostility, from non-computerate colleagues. At first isolated, their efforts have become increasingly coordinated, not least in the UK due to the good offices of CILT (to which the CALL community owes a considerable debt of gratitude) and its intermittently published newsletter CALLBOARD. Even before the advent of the microcomputer, the earliest pioneers braved the hostile environment of the mainframe, but most advances in CALL have taken place in the more accessible and friendly environment of the microcomputer.

Natural languages constitute a notoriously open-ended, wilfully idiosyncratic and hugely complex set of systems, and it might seem at first sight somewhat strange that a modern linguist should even consider turning to a tool which can only cope with a finite, unambiguous and restricted subset of a natural language and which is severely restricted, not only in the pedagogical role it can play, but also in the very narrow range of interactions it offers to the language learner (limited, as it is, largely to written and reading skills).

The potentiality of the computer appears all the more restricted as a language teacher if you couple that to the fact that communicative competence is now increasingly playing a central role at all levels of language learning. I mean no disrespect to its proponents, but I have seen so many language teaching orthodoxies come and go, and I have yet to see a clearly enunciated set of soundly based tenets to support the communicative case. Doubtless it will be established, only to be toppled by a new orthodoxy. Perhaps one day (fond hope), language teaching theoreticians will wake up to the fact that there is no one way of teaching a foreign language, no one approach which guarantees success, and no one exclusive area of language skills which can be isolated and imposed upon the learner.

But I digress. The evidence of much early tutorial-type CALL (or question-and-answer-based CALL) seemed to point in two undesirable directions. First, the emphasis appeared to lie excessively on accuracy, and it is clear that an undue or inappropriate insistence on accuracy for its own sake militates against smooth progress on the part of the learner, and can actually get in the way of the learning process in certain circumstances. The response to that anxiety is that CALL does not have to insist on accuracy, and that bad teaching practice in that direction is by no means limited to poorly designed computer programs. It is simply that, as in the case of structure drills in the language laboratory, question plus accurate response happens to be the easiest kind of test to mount on the computer. A less simplistic level of interaction simply requires a modicum of design ability on the part of the programmer.

A second, and more substantial, objection relates to the kind of skills being tested, and here the objectors are on much firmer ground. First, the learner is being obliged to fumble around the keyboard to find the right keys (and pretty eccentric keys at that, if we are dealing with accented letters). The objection again stands unchallenged only if the program is badly designed. If CALL is going to work at all, some keyboard skills have to be learned (some programs do go to great lengths to minimize the amount of skills to be acquired), and kept within modest bounds, and coupled with the general desirability of becoming familiar with computing equipment, this is no bad thing in itself.

Designers must, however, be aware that if the learner is hunting and pecking about the keyboard in order to type in an excessively long response, the noise-to-signal ratio deteriorates beyond desirable levels. The longer the reponse required becomes, the greater the chance of error, of the learner actually forgetting in his search for a particular key what the answer is that he was typing in, and the more problematical the appropriate processing of that response by the program becomes. So, for all these reasons, in most cases a minimal response within clearly defined parameters is clearly the most desirable option for the program designer to aim for in his CALL packages.

In addition and more importantly, there is the question of the silent micro. This is by far the most substantial objection to the introduction of CALL in its earlier manifestations. The learner types, the screen types back. All this interaction occurs in total silence, save for the clicking of the keyboard, and occasional gratuitous audio bouquets and brickbats pro- grammed into the computer's loudspeaker to accompany the right or wrong responses.

My first response to this objection is yes, of course the computer is silent. So is a book, and no one expects a book to speak. In other words, the image of the computer in the media (and, to be fair, the one which too many in the scientific community who ought to know better are promoting) is of an all- powerful, world-shattering system poised to take over the earth. I may be injecting a touch of hyperbole into the assertion, but it is none the less true that the perception of the computer in the public mind is decades ahead of the reality sitting on the office or classroom desk.

A second response would be that, agreed, the computer is silent, but within those clear limitations it has a role to perform, limited but significant. Additionally, it could be pointed out that the computer is now beginning to speak, both in the computer-controlled cassette recorder, with videodisc, and CDI and CD-ROM. Those technologies are available now, but they are relatively expensive (with the exception of the cassette recorder). There is, too, the potentially much cheaper option of the voice synthesizer, but here the technology limps behind the expectations. As for speech recognition, that lies in the future (how far ahead, one hesitates to guess, but the most reasonable supposition is that it will come later rather than sooner).

So the question remains about the desirability of recruiting the silent micro into language teaching. The teaching of language skills acquisition is an extremely complex business, not only because of the varied nature of the competencies to be inculcated — from the productive skills of speaking, writing, interpreting and the rest, to the receptive skills of reading and listening — but also because of the daunting task of seeking to compress into a relatively short space of time and in competition with other subjects and activities a learning process which native speakers were able to absorb at their own pace, as it were, over a period of many years.

Thus it is that, apart from the occasional detour into blind or well-meaning dogma, the approach of modern language teachers is essentially pragmatic, hence too their willingness to consider enlisting any piece of appropriate equipment into their armoury of teaching tools, although, as indicated earlier, the ranks of the cynics has been swollen by past experiences with the language laboratory. There are two aspects of language skills acquisition which particularly attracted the attention of language teachers to the potential of the computer. The first is the fact that learning rates vary considerably within a student group, not only from one learner to another, but also in one and the same learner when confronted with various tasks at differing levels of ability. This is an especially serious problem, since language learning is — particularly in its earlier stages — essentially a linear and cumulative process: each stage has to be satisfactorily mastered before progress can properly be made to the next. Secondly, language learning is unique in that it demands an *active* knowledge of all the basic semantic and lexical features of the target language: an ability not just to know as a fact a particular feature of a language, but to be able to draw it out of a hat, so to speak, instantaneously and in the correct grammatical form.

These two key aspects of language learning involve the expenditure of considerable time and effort and, beyond a certain point, are not cost-effective for the majority of a class which has both understood and assimilated a particular point, whilst a few individuals lag behind (and potentially further and further behind). Seeing the computer primarily as a potential reinforcing and remedial tool (not as a teacher of new information), the pioneers sought to adapt the machine as a means of releasing the teacher for more effective personal contact with the class group.

2.7   SPECIFIC OBJECTIONS TO CALL

In Chapter 1, we considered objections to the application of technology to language teaching, and having touched on more general concerns about the value of CALL, the time has now come to confront the major objections to the applications of CALL in detail.

There is no denying the commitment and enthusiasm of the proponents of CALL, but it has been argued that the outcome is less than satisfactory. Enthusiasm is not enough. The end products, it has been claimed, have all too frequently displayed the following undesirable features:

(1) a depersonalizing of language teaching;
(2) programs of inferior quality;
(3) inflexible interaction with the learner;
(4) no monitoring or validation;
(5) inappropriate testing methods;
(6) not adaptable to modern methodologies;
(7) no 'intelligent' awareness of either the teacher or the student model.

These are substantial objections, and merit thorough consideration. However, I must say that it does appear that those critical of CALL tend to apply far more rigorous standards of criticism against it than they would if they were approaching other areas of language teaching.

2.7.1 Mechanizing the learning process?

It seems at first sight almost too self-evident to merit consideration that the introduction of CALL has represented an attempt both to mechanize and depersonalize the language teaching process. Instead of direct personal contact with a human teacher, the learner is forced to face a cathode ray tube and interact with it.

The general consensus among language teachers is indeed that there is really no substitute for personal individual interaction as a key constituent element of the language skills acquisition process. Even in relatively small groups, however, the frequency of such interaction will be heavily diluted, especially where one or two learners are experiencing particular difficulties. The computer was envisaged, then, as a remedial tool, as a means of concentrating the intensity of interaction for the learner in difficulty. Instead of being targeted once or twice in a 30-minute session, the learner can be given a response to all his input, and gains the undivided attention of the computer. The quality of that response is, of course, quite a different matter, and one which we shall consider elsewhere.

At the same time, it has been recognized that in the specific context of remedial language work, the very impersonality of the computer, far from being a deterrent to learning, has been a positive advantage. Language teachers tend to be strong and forceful personalities who can all too easily intimidate and overwhelm the shrinking violet struggling to come to terms with some linguistic difficulty, and — as has been noted in medical experiments with first-time patient interaction with a computer terminal — the removal of the human personality from certain kinds of interaction is a positive benefit, especially if the patient is experiencing pain in a location which it is not socially acceptable to mention in polite company.

The other side of the coin is that targeting specific problem areas for individual learners both enables the general pace of learning to be maintained for the whole group, without the learner with difficulties falling further and further behind, and in general terms many CALL workers report both an increase in motivation generally on the part of students and, too, a feeling that there is more time to concentrate on activities which further promote the learning process. I cite just one example by way of illustration:

> I feel it has contributed to some of my students' more accurate performance and in their greater confidence. These students seem to share my feelings. It has, furthermore, allowed me to devote more of my class time to other activities and to consolidate those aspects of the language that are conceptual and must be understood before they are memorised. (Bentley, 1987, p. 134.)

As you will have recognized, most such benefits are perceived as coming in the early stages of learning a language, particularly when *ab initio* learners are being placed under pressure to bring their knowledge up to a high level in a short space of time.

2.7.2   The quality of programs

There is no disputing the fact that early packages for CALL contained examples of programming of a less than admirable quality. There are, however, a number of mitigating factors to be considered, the most important of which is that these early programs were largely written, not by computer experts writing to order, but by experts in the applications subject operating in a much more critical environment than computer programmers are accustomed to find themselves in. In addition, the pioneers had no inhibitions in demonstrating their wares, however inadequate.

It should further be recognized that the blemishes characterizing these programs were marginal rather than fundamental, and due either to inexperience in computer programming (for example, not catering for the learner who inadvertently — or deliberately — presses the ESCAPE or BREAK key while a package is running), or inexperience in designing computer software at a quite advanced level (for example, coping with a cocktail of upper and lower case input, or with alternative answers, or superfluous punctuation keyed in by the learner). Those dismissive of early CALL failed to recognize the fact that these were not crucial blunders, merely symptoms of the now well-recognized fact that CALL involves the acquisition by the teacher of expertise in areas as diverse as computer programming, software design, the user interface, software psychology, and much more. On top of that, design improvement depends crucially in CALL as in many other fields on extensive field testing, not least because CALL was then — and is now — breaking entirely new territory.

2.7.3   Inflexible interaction

The insistence on absolute accuracy, it is argued, is bad enough, but when the program asks for the German for 'car', and will accept only 'Wagen', not 'Auto' (let alone 'Automobil' or even 'Kraftfahrzeug'), then the learner is being badly taught and loses respect for the mechanical tutor. Both these situations can be ameliorated by various software design techniques — they are emphatically not weaknesses inbuilt in the system.

It is a straightforward process to accommodate alternative answers and help information in a tutorial package, and there are several well-designed such packages in existence. If you seek to move beyond that level to finding ways of accepting nearly right answers, you admittedly will find yourself in an increasing tangle of complexities, particularly if you sought to devise a general algorithm to cope with such responses:

> What if the routine accepted transposed letters? This would not be so serious with 'dreiunddriessig', perhaps, but 'furchtbar' (frightful) and 'fruchtbar' (fruitful) could be a fatal error, as could 'cieling' in a test of the 'i before e' rule in English. (Last, 1984, p. 39.)

And you would be in equally serious difficulties, but for different reasons, if your list of 'nearly right' responses were tailor-made for a particular response:

> If we were to make the net as wide as possible, it would mean dozens of possible checks, plus at least one unique error message, for just one French word. And unless the net is capable of catching all these possibilities, the computer can be made to look stupid — the worst possible position for a teacher to be in, particularly when the teacher is a machine. (Jacobs, 1988, p. 15.)

And there is a third category of error, which even the human teacher finds it very hard indeed to detect, namely, when a learner gets the right answer (or the correct lexical form) for the wrong reasons, where, for example, 'sich' in German is dative form and the learner perceives it to be accusative.

Which brings me back to the excessively high standards of criticism applied by some opponents of CALL. We must be aware of all the limitations of CALL, and must seek to push those limitations as far as possible, but so long as the learner is quite clear as to what the nature of the limitations are in a CALL exercise, there is no pedagogical demerit in their existence.

Provided that the learner knows that this exercise requires the verb to be in the perfect tense, or that the answers are all case-sensitive (in the computing sense, that is, of upper and lower case being significant), or whatever the preconditions are, then the 'limitations' themselves become a positive benefit in that they spell out clearly the parameters within which the interaction occurs, and that helps to render the interaction more stable and less open-ended or uncertain for the learner, particularly one who is experiencing particular learning problems in this area.

2.7.4 No monitoring or validation

The presence or absence of monitoring procedures is purely and simply a matter of program design. In some situations, the learner is best left to commit blunders without the fear of an electronic big brother peering over his shoulder, in others it is valuable to keep a record of student performance. Of course, it has to be a meaningful record, not, as in the case of some packages I have seen, merely a bald statement to the effect that X or Y had so many attempts at such-and-such and scored Z per cent, which is pretty meaningless information.

Evidence of the potency of monitoring at a fairly sophisticated level goes back to the early days of CALL. In a beginners' Dutch course in the University of Hull using the EXERCISE package which I had designed, King integrated CALL into each learning module, and the computer print-out of student performance (which crucially included details of all the wrong responses) formed part of the basis of the summing-up phase of each course module. As King points out:

> This analysis of the individual student's performance can be very rapidly retrieved from a weekly lineprinter listing of errors under user names .... The greatest asset in the error data analysis is its immediate and up-to-date availability. This means that students are aware that their work is being followed through day by day and can be discussed with them almost up to the moment of the tutorial in which problems are dealt with. (Last and King, 1979, pp. 196–197.)

As to the evaluatory objection, it is true that it is notoriously difficult to quantify the merits of one approach rather than another, and language teachers tend to be far too busy (and concerned about the best interests of their students) to set up experiments with control groups and the like. From my own personal experience (however unreliable you may regard that) and from extensive discussions with CALL practitioners, it emerges unambiguously that, while the language laboratory can be confidently said not to cause actual clinical damage to health yet its benefits remain nebulous to say the least, CALL increases the motivation and interest level of students, particularly in the more tiresome aspects of language learning (drilling and transformations), and that this effect persists long after the novelty of the computer wears off.

King confirms that 'the console threatens neither the tedium nor the confusion associated with the listening booth' (Last and King, 1979, p. 196), and the evidence in the literature points generally in the direction of positive reactions, even given the extremely primitive level of some of the CALL material described.

There have, in fact, been some 'consumer surveys' conducted in CALL projects, which tend to take the form of questionnaires to be filled in by the learner at certain stages in the project. As in the case of one Arabic CALL teaching programme, positive reactions to the course were matched by specific criticisms of points of weakness which the teachers were able to design out of the system (see Brockett, 1987). Another project, this time in Spanish, elicited a similar response (Bentley, 1987).

2.7.5   Teaching the wrong things the wrong way

I have already considered the questions of the over-emphasis of accuracy, and the lack of a speaking voice or listening ear on the part of the computer. The main objection in this category comes from those who are wedded to an orthodoxy antipathetical to 'drilling' as a means of bridging the unique gap in language learning between passive and active assimilation of information. To know 'for a fact' that the French for house is 'maison' is a quite different, and less demanding, matter than being able to draw the word 'maison' out of the mind in the correct gender, form, position and context in a split second together with all the other linguisitic components constituting a spoken utterance in the foreign language, and drilling is one means towards achieving that end.

If one is aware — and what language teacher is not? — of the twin dangers of learning the sequence in which the answers come rather than the words themselves (the learner who has to recite 'je suis', and so on, in order to arrive at the third person plural is no better than the learner who has to chant right through the table to end up at 12 times 6) and of isolating the drilling process in a non-contextualized situation, then drilling in my view has a substantial and positive role to play. Learners are anxious to drill themselves as part of the process of gaining confidence in their language acquisition skills, and many CALL practitioners have pointed sadly to the fact that learners, like the child at Christmas opting for the cheap teddy bear and ignoring the computerized train set, tend to scorn the more complex forms of interaction offered by sophisticated packages, and turn time and again (for comfort?) to what even their designers regard as mindless drilling routines. Perhaps we as teachers have a lesson to learn from our students in this regard.

2.7.6 Failing to cope with modern approaches to teaching
Tutorial CALL in particular is all too often regarded as the creature of the drill and practice associated with traditional grammar-based approaches to modern languages teaching. There is no truth in this assertion whatsoever. The designers of software packages of all kinds have demonstrated time and again that the applicability, even of tutorial-type CALL, is very wide indeed, and it can be applied across a vast range of different areas of language teaching.

The multiple choice question has been turned into an adventure-type game in Jacobs's *French on the run* (Jacobs, 1987), there are any number of packages specifically designed to test inferencing ability in a variety of ways (Wida Software's *Storyboard*, or *Context* by Lewis) — and so the list could continue more or less indefinitely. For recent software release information, see CALLBOARD from NCCALL. In the next section, we shall be considering a number of examples of good CALL practice.

Successful inroads have even been made into the more challenging area of communicative competence, the latest fashion in language teaching. There is a description of an ingenious role-playing package in French by Atkinson in Heath (1987), which clearly demonstrates the flexibility of quite simple kinds of interaction with the learner, and, interestingly, here too one of the perceived benefits of the packages is that of encouraging 'those pupils who are reticent or hesitant in role-play work' (Heath, 1987, p. 47).

2.7.7 No 'intelligent' awareness
Again, one aspect of this objection has already been sufficiently aired. The computer should not necessarily be expected to evince intelligence just because the media hype claims it to be the great megabrain of the future. As Fodor rightly underlines, the assumption that a computer could or should be capable of intelligence remains at the very least unproven:

> If someone . . . were to ask us why we should even suppose that the digital computer is a plausible mechanism for the simulation of

global cognitive processes, the answering silence would be deafening. (Fodor, 1983, p. 129.)

There is, however, another aspect of the intelligence objection raised against current CALL, and it is one worthy of consideration. The objection goes like this: the computer responds in the same way to each and every learner, and fails to distinguish intelligently between different current levels of performance and ability. Again, one response would be that we do not expect a book to react differently to different readers. Nor, I would argue, is it essential for a computer to do so, even if it possesses the potentiality to move in this direction.

There is a very practical reason for this, and that is the common feature in educational technology of escalating input in terms of time and effort for diminishing returns. A fairly simple program offering a modest level of interaction can be put together without the expenditure of excessive time and effort, but each additional benefit (if benefit it be) demands an escalating input for an increasingly marginal amount of return. This does not mean that I am opposed in any way to moulding the interaction in such a way that it acquires, and acts upon, a model of the learner. One could, in fact, argue that this occurs at a vestigial level in the most modest of packages, by the learner himself choosing exercise number five, since he has already polished off exercises one to four. Indeed, in my EXERCISE package which I designed for the mainframe environment, the drills were based on a large number of short exercises progressing in difficulty, each supported by back-up exercises for the learner with problems.

Two results emerged from this approach: first, the learner benefited from being able to choose, rather than being forced by the computer into jumping through particular learning hoops because the machine perceived the learner as not competent to proceed to the next learning phase. Secondly, from the design point of view, it soon emerged that even at this modest level of sophistication, a substantial effort in designing and keying in exercises was required in order, in some cases, to cover eventualities which might never arise. In any given year, there may well be a number of backup exercises which are never summoned up at all. So the cost effectiveness of the undertaking has to be a matter of scrutiny. One option here, of course, is for the learner to request a backup exercise, and if it is not available on-line, an exercise can be written as required. But the general message again is that of research enthusiasm running away with and from the practicalities of the situation. And, too, there is an element which we shall be returning to in relation to AI itself; namely, demanding that the computer be more comprehensive and perfect in its performance than either its human programmer or any other learning technology devised by human beings.

2.7.8 Examples of good CALL practice
The first principle, and the one on which everything else in CALL should be founded, is that of the integrity of the relationship between computer and

learner. At first reading, that might well sound a curious statement to those unfamiliar with CALL, but it can never be repeated too often that we are, as far as the learner is concerned, not embarking on some fancy adventure into technology, but simply extending the teaching and learning process into another appropriate area which just happens to be that of computing.

In all teaching and learning situations, a relationship based on a mixture of trust, confidence, mutual respect, and responsiveness should exist between the teacher on the one hand and the learner on the other. If the computer cannot be programmed to perform adequately on these counts, then we might as well abandon all hope of creating any kind of computer–learner interaction and freeze technological progress at the chalkboard and the overhead projector.

Without wishing to identify and name a product which contains such serious deficiencies (which can be readily overcome), I cite an imaginary example which is based on a commercially available product from an extremely prestigious source. I have changed the language involved.

One of the programs within the package presents on the screen a series of anagrams which the learner is invited to unscramble. Other deficiencies apart, the programmers have failed to take the precaution of ensuring that a random scrambling of the letters of a particular word does not result in them emerging by happenstance in exactly the same order as the answer. The learner has every right to expect that an anagram will be a genuine re-ordering of an individual word. Let us leave aside the relatively minor glitches that (a) a word, say 'trap', might be scrambled into another genuine word, say 'part'; or (b) that a learner might opt for 'part' as the correct answer when the program only knows 'trap' as right.

The relationship of trust between learner and teacher breaks down when the teacher is shown to be inadequate or unreliable. It is also imperilled at the point at which communication between the two appears to break down.

2.8   BEST PRACTICE IN FIRST-GENERATION CALL

Let it not be thought, however, that there is little of merit in currently available commercial CALL. This is far from being true, and it is worth briefly considering some of the better quality packages that are available in order to demonstrate both that good material, well researched and presented, is available, and that the mode of interaction with the learner is far from being exclusively that of tutorial-type question and answer sequences.

The purpose of this section is to give a flavour of the wide range of good material that is currently available, and to present this as the current state of the art in the sense that it is from this kind of launch pad that any serious advances in CALL must occur.

I take by way of illustration packages which are commercially available at the time of writing, and which are likely to find their way into the modern languages departments of schools and colleges.

2.8.1   The 'Master' series

I turn first to a suite of packages which have been around for a long time, and in fact number among the earliest CALL packages. Now available for the PC and compatibles, the 'Master' series of authoring packages cover the most familiar ground of first-generation CALL. Choicemaster is perhaps the simplest of all the packages: it enables the teacher to set up a series of multiple choice exercises. There is nothing startlingly innovative about that, of course, and I shall refrain from rehearsing the familiar arguments for and against this mode of testing. The package is however constructed with considerable care and attention to detail, demonstrating that even the most modest form of tutorial-type interaction can be turned into a meaningful educational environment for the learner.

Opportunities are built in for the teacher to incorporate comments explaining why answers are wrong, and there is a feature which enables the learner to browse through a completed exercise and review his performance. Even at this straightforward level, then, it is possible to create material of educational merit without there being any suggestion that it is in any way 'intelligent'. It is an extension of a pen and paper based exercise given the added dimension of a modest degree of interaction with the designer of the exercise.

Of all the packages in this suite, the one that offers the most for the language learner is the 'Storyboard' package, which tests a skill which, I feel, is much underrated in language learning, and that is inferencing ability. A text is placed on the screen in the form of a series of blobs representing individual letters, gaps, and punctuation marks. The learner is then offered a number of different strategies for translating the screen into the text upon which it is based. Attempts can be made at inserting whole words throughout the text — obvious candidates in English would be 'the', 'and', 'but' and other connectives — or individual letters, and so forth. As in any teaching situation, of course, the success of the exercise depends on the designing skills of the teacher. Where a passage depends for comprehension on a date, place name or other such factor which may not be reasonably inferred from the context, difficulties will inevitably arise. But a well-designed exercise of this nature offers a more than acceptable paradigm for good practice in first-generation CALL.

2.8.2   A 'bookware' package

The next package under consideration, Viewbook.Author, represents a well-constructed implementation of the concept of 'bookware'. It is a notion which is not specifically designed for foreign language teaching, but is one which can readily be applied for that purpose. The package is an authoring system which allows you to create, effectively, a book on a disk, with the normal structure of contents list, chapters, pages within chapters, and an index. The chief limitation within which the system functions is that the information presented should be so formulated that it can be output in screen-sized units, which is a good discipline for the presentation of factual information, but does pose problems if the text is any form of creative writing.

The great benefit of this system is that it exploits the flexibility of the computer in enabling the reader to go to any part of the 'book', to use the index and refer instantly to the appropriate page or pages, to follow cross-references pre-edited by the author, to search at a moderately sophisticated level through the text and index, and additionally to offer the reader a notepad facility on screen.

Here, clearly, is an environment which offers a high degree of flexibility and interaction on a number of different levels without straying at all from the conventional notion of first-generation CALL. It also has the merit of enabling the learner to have control of the learning process without the risk of falling into the more serious dangers presented by learner-directed education. This, then, is what I am tempted to designate as 'classic' CALL at its best, despite a claim in the manual to the effect that this represents a form of hypertext (which we shall be considering in a later chapter), which it is not.

2.8.3   Instant correspondence
This is an ingenious application of CALL which operates in a number of different languages. Entitled 'Tick-Tack' from Primrose publishing, it consists of a number of 'building block' sentences which can be applied in the construction of correspondence on a business level. The sentences are coded, and you summon up a sentence in the appropriate foreign language simply by typing in a series of codes.

The resulting output can then be modified to suit the particular circumstances for which you are writing. Again, ingenuity on the part of the package designer has succeeded in stretching CALL into an attractive aid in teaching commercial aspects of foreign languages.

2.8.4   The German sentence builder
The most adventurous package to be considered here was written by Ian Johnston with two particular objectives in mind: the first was to design a learning environment at the sentence level which avoided the necessity for a measure of keyboard skills; the second was to push as far as possible the notion of an 'intelligent' interaction with the learner without resorting to the familiar tutorial mode.

The concept enables German sentences to be typed in by the teacher consisting of subject, tensed main-clause verb, indirect and direct objects, past participles or infinitives, and time, manner and place phrases. The learner then manipulates these phrases on the screen to construct a German sentence in an acceptable word order. There is considerable help available, and the whole object of the package is to seek to operate at the sentence level rather than that of the individual word or phrase.

2.9   CONCLUSION
The present best practice first of all acknowledges the limitations of the medium, secondly, seeks to operate well within those limitations, and

thirdly, offers a lively and interesting mode of interaction with the learner which supplements the role of the teacher in an effective and positive manner. It is through material such as this that, in my view, one of the most important functions of CALL can be performed; namely, that of permitting the teacher to concentrate on the key areas of foreign language teaching, in which human–human interaction is the only possible and meaningful mode, and in that interaction for the teacher to be able to concentrate more on advancing the learners' knowledge of the subject than on a concern for those who, for one reason or another, are falling behind, failing to comprehend a particular concept, and thereby holding back the others in the group.

At the same time, of course, such CALL material can be employed as an additional stimulus to the more gifted learner. Thus it is that the best practice in current CALL serves the double purpose of remedial teaching on the one hand and of extending the learner on the other, provided only that it remains within the limitations prescribed by the programming techniques and the technology.

3

What is AI?

Whole books have been written about AI, even about narrow specific aspects of AI. So this chapter in no way aspires to being a comprehensive survey of the development and current state of the art of AI. For such an account, I recommend Partridge (1986) and Haugeland (1985).

What I have sought to do is to state the broad issues of AI in general terms as they relate to the theme of this book, and to draw out some of the major problems — paradoxes, even — inherent in those problems. AI as a subject has engendered as much passion as any highly controversial scientific investigation, and perhaps even more so than in any other area, since AI is all about modelling the human mind, mimicking intelligent behaviour, creating a working brain that functions like our own, but possibly without the weaknesses that hamper our thought processes.

In western society, we are conditioned to believe in the possibility, indeed the inevitability, of progress as the placing of one brick upon another until a new edifice is constructed which in turn serves as the basis for the next advance. AI (to date, at least) has not quite turned out like that. To set the scene, here is an observation by Haugeland which can serve to lay out the agenda for much of this chapter:

> AI ... is based on a powerful idea, which very well might be right (or right in some respects) and just as well might not. (Haugeland, 1985.)

The key point of this observation is that AI is not like the motor car, which exists and functions to specification, but which is capable of more and more refinement and development. AI has not yet arrived. It is more like the dreams of past centuries of powered flight, an aspiration which may one day become reality. Whether AI ever actually takes off or not is still largely a matter for conjecture.

3.1 STATING THE PROBLEM

In the popular mind, AI almost invariably tends to be perceived as a single, monolithic field of scientific investigation. This misconception inevitably leads to a considerable degree of blurring and over-simplification of the issues involved. In addition, AI tends to be invested with an unwarranted aura of glamour, which may be useful in attracting funding or television appearances, but does little to disguise the fact that this is a science (some would argue, an art) which is very much in its infancy, and showing little signs of being able to make a breakthrough into the very difficult areas which have to be conquered if it is to become a practical proposition in assisting man to control his environment.

It is important to recognize, as Haugeland states, that AI is an 'idea', an objective which may never be attained. AI does not describe an actuality which is alive and well and living amongst us.

In fact, there is no one single, clearly defined subject area with an exclusive claim to the title 'artificial intelligence'. AI spreads across a very wide range of different disciplines embracing, for example, engineering, philosophy, linguistics, and psychology, and covers a number of very divergent AI 'end products', from robotics, expert systems, problem-solving and game-playing programs, and other undertakings which can be bracketed under the heading of 'applications' of AI, to what might be termed 'pure' AI at the other end of the spectrum, in other words, using the computer as a tool for modelling the mind and investigating the highly complex processes of the human brain. In addition, it is worth recording that although much effort is now devoted to the implementation of AI programs on the computer, AI is not inevitably wedded to the computer. It can and does exist as a concept apart from the machine.

The confusion is worse confounded by the fact that no one, even the most committed AI researcher, appears to be able to set out in clear and undisputed terms what, precisely, 'intelligence' is, nor indeed how it can effectively be expressed through the medium of the electronic digital computer, of whatever generation. As a non-scientist observing the great AI debate, I find most confusing of all the fact that opinions are so sharply divided as to the genuine potential and actual achievements of AI. I tend to take the line that, when opinions are so divergent and there is no clear leading view or set of views, the most logical conclusion to draw is not that one of the views is correct but that all of them are wrong to some degree or other.

Before we can begin to consider how, if at all, AI techniques are applicable in CALL, it is important to gain a general overview of the perceptions of AI among scientists as well as, to some extent at least, its place in the public consciousness, in order to be able to mark out how the most apposite starting point for taking CALL a step forward might be determined. Further, it is necessary to acquire an understanding of the actual state of the art and the context within which AI researchers are currently working if we are to build upon present achievements rather than, as happened in the early days of CALL, taking too much of a leap backwards to first principles and starting from a point well below the level of the state of the art in other subject areas.

So first, let us turn to a consideration of perceptions of AI. In what follows, I shall follow the practice of my scientific colleagues of occasionally talking in terms of the 'computer' when I refer both to the hardware and/or to the software that drives it. This is, I feel, a reasonable compromise long since struck by the computer scientist between pedantry on the one hand and sloppy usage on the other.

Let me start with my own perception, which is as fallible as that of others but which it is important to spell out, since it forms the basis of my attitude towards the application of AI in CALL and therefore very much colours the way in which the rest of this book has been written. In my view, people are people and machines are machines. I find it odd that there are strong scientific pressures to make computing machines more and more like people when the first priority ought to be to make those machines better at being machines.

Futurology is a hazardous pursuit at the best of times, but it does none the less seem to me rather quixotic to claim that computing systems as we know them can be developed to the point at which they can perform like human beings and to interact with human beings on equal terms. Leaving aside the desirability or otherwise of a machine behaving like a fallible, error-prone human being at all, there is an evident and irresolvable conflict between programming systems as we currently know and apply them and the concept of the 'ideal' AI program. Present techniques of non-AI programming involve spelling out the problem in advance, defining it rigorously in every detail, and designing strong algorithms to ensure that the right results are obtained every time. An AI program is by definition almost the very antithesis of conventional deterministic programming: the AI problem is by its very nature ill-defined, the algorithms weak, driven by probabilities at best rather than by certainties, and the objective is not accurate and dependable, but rather, adequate performance.

This does not signify that I am 'opposed' to the notion of AI, rather that I err on the side of extreme caution in a field in which aspiration and speculation abound, but in which hard actual results are meagre in the extreme. I am also particularly concerned at the devaluation of concepts of 'intelligence'. It is clear, for example, that the much-quoted MYCIN program in medical science which acts as an expert system in medical diagnosis (of which more later) is not in any real sense intelligent, although large claims have been made for the inroads which such programs are supposedly making into the domains of AI. MYCIN does no more than manipulate 'numerically weighted associations between observable manifestations and disease hypotheses'. (Knipers, 1987, p. 708.) In other words, the programs can cope with no more than surface-level information. The computer 'knows' nothing about the underlying principles of the pieces of information which it is manipulating. It is blindly manipulating symbols (albeit in a fairly sophisticated manner) according to a set of principles which have been fed into it in advance.

A recent paper on knowledge abstraction points to what are perceived to be 'some very definite limitations on the knowledge than can be represented in computer programs'. The nature of the limitation is expressed in these terms:

> In general, computers cannot know things by virtue of not being
> able to experience them. Without such knowledge a computer
> cannot abstract symbolic knowledge that is based on experience or
> abilities. (Abbott, 1987, p. 669.)

In other words, a significant and essential part of intelligent behaviour is conditioned by our ability to feel physical and emotional sensations: heat, cold, love and hate. The absence of such potentiality in present computing machinery critically inhibits their ability to perform in an intelligent manner. You may, of course, adopt a rationalist approach and assert that the isolation of intelligence (if it can be isolated) from the human experience will enable a computing system to come to its decisions in a more detached and rational manner. But a moment's thought will dismiss that fallacy. Intelligent behaviour includes avoiding life-threatening physical phenomena, like a raging fire or an icy stream, and the emotions play a significant role in arriving at difficult judgements in a whole range of different spheres. A computerized judge could scarcely arrive at a judgement of Solomon without emotional awareness and maturity.

This recognition of the severe limitations of the computer in relation to intelligent behaviour is far from being an isolated view expressed by a handful of Luddites seeking to hold back the next logical step forward in the progress of technology. The stance is expressed even more forcefully by Carroll and McKendree in terms which underpin my own attitude towards 'AI programs':

> Philosophers can rest easy; for today's computers to 'have know-
> ledge' means no more than to be able to store information and act
> on the basis of that information. (Carroll and McKendree, 1987, p.
> 15.)

As we shall see at a later stage, the real focal point of the debate as far as AI and CALL are concerned does not lie in the concept of intelligence as a human characteristic which may or may not be capable of being distilled and broken down into its component parts, if indeed it is possible to achieve that objective:

> Intelligence is widely believed to be the product of evolution and
> hence it is reassuring to know that it is perhaps likely to be
> decomposable into a modular hierarchy. But although we thus have
> some reason to hope that intelligence is a modular phenomenon, we
> still have to find the modules. (Partridge, 1986, p. 37.)

Our concern will focus on 'applied intelligence', the behaviour of the human expert and the attempt to develop parallel intelligent computer programs, expert systems. The same paradox of modularity is to be found in expert behaviour as it is in relation to intelligence in general. While an expert can be said to perform in a specific problem domain in a highly efficient manner, it has so far proved to be a far from trivial undertaking to boil that expert behaviour down into its basic component parts, so that they can then be rebuilt in terms which a computer program can master.

And when — or if — computers advance to the point at which they can be said to be sufficiently humanoid to be permitted to perform some more advanced human roles, there will have to take place a moral debate as searching as the one currently being conducted in the spheres of genetic engineering and experimentation of various kinds on the live human foetus *in vitro*. But that is to rush into an unknown and as yet unpredictable future.

Let us come down to earth: on the basis of current AI research and programming results, it is clear that progress towards that kind of 'ideal', if ideal it be, has been minimal. The present most fruitful line of investigation for AI-based programming in CALL, then, seems to lie along the path of data-driven programs which venture into the sphere of probabilities and possibilities rather than certainties. To attempt anything grander than that at this stage of the state of the art may well be more than a little foolish.

But I turn now to consider the two most widely held views of AI, since it is important both to be aware of the nature and impact of these attitudes and to be able to distill fact from fancy before we seek to determine which techniques are practical possibilities. In what follows, I consider three basic attitudes towards AI: the ardent proponents, who envision a new computer age of thinking machines as being well within our grasp; the equally strong opponents of the notion that AI is either realizable or desirable; and a middle view, which while being neither excessively optimistic nor pessimistic, takes a pragmatic approach of applying those achievements which have been made and building on them in a step-by-step approach.

3.2 THE 'OPTIMISTIC' VIEW OF AI

At one extreme, the computer is perceived as being poised to take over the world. It is taken for granted by many scientists that there is a natural progression from the current state of the computing art via an upward hardware path to fifth-generation machines and an upward software path to real AI programs which will interact in 'natural language' with us humans. There is, in the view of the AI optimists, as I might call them, a continuum between the present state of the art of AI and the goal or objective of the intelligent machine. It is simply a matter of time and research before the gap between aspiration and reality is closed.

The optimistic lobby has produced some astonishingly unscientific books, epitomized by the breathtakingly overwritten *Machines who think*, which concludes on this jarring note:

> And so with the reflexive enterprise of artificial intelligence. We are as gods in the exercise, counterfeiting aspects of the human just as we always have, whether in theology or the arts, and for pretty much the same reasons of self-enchantment. That we might be forging the gods in the other sense — deities to rescue us from our

own overreaching — is an idea allowing degrees of accord. (McCorduck, 1979, p. 357.)

The view that we might justifiably be daring to fetch a new fire from
heaven judiciously glosses over the awkward practical details as to how it
might be achieved.

But perhaps the most extreme representative of this AI triumphalism is
encapsulated in the extraordinary book *Are computers alive? Evolution and
new life forms*, which I am more than tempted to believe was published on 1
April. It is tempting to dismiss this kind of work as the computing equivalent
of the 'looney left', and as such to be regarded as having no place in the
mainstream academic debate about the future developmental path of the
computing machine. But I include a critique of this book for two reasons.
First, it reflects the kind of perception of the computer which the media
seems anxious to impress into the lay public mind. And secondly, it is really
no more than an attempt to follow through to their logical conclusions many
of the precepts held by less extreme AI optimists.

In this prolegomenon to the computer takeover of the world, the author
Simons writes of *machina sapiens*:

> Computer life has been prefigured over the centuries in mythology,
> theatre, and film: imaginative and creative people have always been
> able to envisage the day when artificial life would appear on Earth.
> (Simons, 1983, p. 29.)

I understand that the same also holds true of fairies and the little people,
but I do not anticipate their imminent appearance amongst ordinary
mortals. If Simons is actually being serious, the kindest dismissal of his views
is that they are attributable to a meek acceptance of the kind of lexical non
sequitur which argues that, if we use the term 'intelligent', then we must be
positing the existence of an actual intelligence:

> Today the literature is full of references to intelligent peripherals
> and terminals, machine intelligence, artificial intelligence. (Simons,
> 1983, p. 28.)

The same argument is applied to the term 'generations'. If the develop
ment of computers can be described in terms of generations, that signifies
that 'there is an evolutionary process from one generation to the next'
(Simons, 1983, p. 58), in a genuinely parallel manner to the literal biological
sense of generation, and the natural evolutionary processes which that
implies. To be rather unkind, I wonder if the term 'smart' terminals (smart is
a synonym for intelligent in this context) indicates the imminent arrival of
the well-dressed computer?

The line of argument has all the insidious persuasiveness of the Piagetan
child anthropomorphizing a cloud or a coloured ball. Simons argues that,
because mathematics, for example, was once regarded as purely a human
area of excellence, but is now performed more swiftly and accurately by

computer, computers are therefore approaching the point at which they will take over the dominant role on this planet.

I presume Simons is again being serious when he asserts in the face of all the evidence of the vast complexity of the 'simplest' life forms at the cellular level and below:

> When compared with lichens or slugs, undisputed life-forms, the emerging robot/computer life-forms are already highly evolved. (Simons, 1983, p. 118.)

Simons manages to persuade himself that the new species, the computer, is already alive on our planet and is just on the verge of being recognized as such. He insidiously shifts the ground on which he argues in order to suit his case, and couples this logical slipperiness with a naive and literal acceptance of the way in which metaphorical usage — like generation, intelligence and so forth — has been applied in the computing context with no more literal or sinister intent than in any other field of human activity.

The argument is, however, more than just another example of misconstruing a quite normal human characteristic, namely, of describing the unfamiliar (computer programs) in terms of the familiar (human conduct) and drawing false analogies between the two. In a later book, the core of the argument is stated thus:

> But a first-generation stored program computer could do differential equations. A dog that could do as much would be regarded as highly intelligent. (Simons, 1988, p. 98.)

Simons misses the point completely. In a well-defined problem domain with context-free rules, it is relatively straightforward to design a program to manipulate those rules within certain strict constraints. Coping with a closed micro-world such as this is light years away from a really intelligent activity. Partridge states the case in a nutshell when he describes a little-admired example of successful adaptive behaviour:

> Traditionally we do not marvel at the knowledge-guided problem solving abilities of a menial worker, or to take that other much-maligned super problem solver, the housewife. It is an undisputable fact that the cleaning of a house requires a large, more diverse, and complex knowledge base than does the playing of international standard chess. Yet success in the latter pursuit is typically taken to be indicative of intelligence whilst the former is rated as a menial chore. (Partridge, 1986, p. 59.)

For those who remain unconvinced, this matter will be explored in some depth in due course.

Typical of the extreme optimistic view of AI is the unsupported assertion which brushes aside difficulties of whatever magnitude and gazes beyond to the golden future. It is couched in terms of what I call the 'not yet' (but coming very soon) approach to AI. Simons provides one example among many:

There are already commercial natural-language systems available, but many of the problems associated with linguistics have not yet been solved. (Simons, 1988, p. 152.)

Simons is far from being alone in this intellectual tortuosity, and its insidious persuasiveness smacks too much of the allure of certain extreme political philosophies for my comfort. Papert and Minsky are among the other leading names in the optimist camp. I conclude this section with one asseveration on the future of the computer which betrays its intellectual shallowness by being seemingly unaware of the irony lurking in the references to the philosopher's stone:

To create a machine intelligence is to seek the philosopher's stone of computer technology. Its achievement will lead to a new order of capability in handling intellectual complexity. (Pohl, 1981, p. 289.)

I turn now to consider why it is that we are so readily lured by the attraction of the machine into an acceptance of the inevitability of mechanical and electronic progress to the point of creating an automaton in our own likeness. The fear for and sneaking admiration of the Frankenstein monster has a considerable hold over us, and it is the purpose of the next section to try to come to terms with our evident obsession in the West with this creative aberration.

3.3   WESTERN FASCINATION WITH THE MACHINE

One issue which has tended to have become rather lost in the debate about whether AI is (a) possible or (b) desirable, but which is none the less crucial to an understanding of whether or not AI can be achieved, is that of our attitude to the machine and mechanical processes in western culture. It is one which the computing optimists seem to take for granted as being the normal attitude to adopt to mechanisms of whatever kind.

We are all familiar with the Victorian infatuation with what have been called 'strong machines', a lasting testament to which can be witnessed in the temples of steam such as Bristol Temple Meads and St Pancras railway stations and many more such enduring artefacts. Strong machines doing work for the benefit of mankind are in the vanguard of progress, and although the concept of industrial growth marching on *ad infinitum* has been increasingly challenged at the margin by green political parties and ecologists pointing a warning finger at the worldwide effects of the shrinking rain forests or the release of chlorofluorocarbons into the atmosphere, we are still as a civilization far from outgrowing our longstanding love affair with the machine. This has become inextricably entangled in our culture with the pursuit of progress in all aspects of our lives as both desirable and inevitable.

Now that affair has been given a strong boost by the advent of the computer, the 'smart machine', which now penetrates into every corner of our lives, and which threatens (if you are a pessimist) or promises to take over more and more of the humdrum and not so humdrum tasks facing humanity and indeed to advance beyond that into a decision-making role.

Roszack is particularly strong in his condemnation of our weaknesses in this respect:

> The computer is the latest episode in this scientific infatuation with mechanistic metaphors borrowed from smart machines. Once again, as in the age of Newton, the scientists need to be reminded that the organisms (human beings) which came before mechanisms are far more remarkable pieces of work than the tools they may occasionally invent when they are not spending their time singing songs, making jokes, telling tales, or worshipping God. (Roszack, 1986, pp. 40–41.)

To pursue this notion a little more closely: there is a clear parallel here, which the reader with a language and literature background will readily recognize, with the distinctive and different perceptions of the experience of fiction in child and adult. A child at a given developmental stage cannot distinguish between the reality and the fiction, whereas one of the corner-stones of creative writing for the adult is that he or she can suspend disbelief, as it were, and enter a fictional world peopled by representatives of '*homo fictus*' (to borrow E. M. Forster's famous phrase) and driven by a strong causality alien to the reality of everyday life. At the end of the reading (or theatrical performance, or whatever), the adult re-emerges into reality from that fictional world and is capable of keeping the two distinct in his mind.

I am not proposing a resurrection of Aristotelian concepts of art by the back door, but it does seem more than likely that a similar pattern is to be observed in relation to machines and inanimate objects generally, but unlike the case of creative art, we as adults appear less able to separate the fiction from the reality.

Piaget, whose views on cognitive development proposed among other things that the child develops from the first stage of self-awareness via the recognition of the concrete world beyond the self to an adult ability to deal with abstractions, took the view that the young child invests inanimate objects beyond the self with a psychology of a kind.

Without wishing to become involved in the debate as to the extent to which this personification and injection of volition into inanimate objects tends to reflect deficiencies in linguistic competency rather than a genuine belief on the child's part in the animism of objects, there is, it seems to me, a considerable body of evidence that the tendency to anthropomorphize the computer extends far beyond the bounds of the child's propensity to infuse life into clouds, toys, or household objects, and impacts on adult perceptions of what is, after all, no more than a box full of wires, printed circuit boards and engraved silicon chips.

Sherry Turkle, in a perceptive analysis of the attitudes of children to the computer, expresses the notion of the computer as an object invested with psychology in these terms:

My major finding here is that physical criteria dominate the discussion of the aliveness of traditional (noncomputational) objects until they give way to standard biological criteria (breathing, growing, metabolism), while psychological criteria dominate the discussion about computational objects for young children and persist even after the child consistently uses biological language to talk about the aliveness of traditional objects. (Turkle, 1984, p. 344.)

Our perception of the computer, then, is conditioned by our attempts to understand it in terms of a thinking machine. This stance is important in relation to the HCI (human–computer interface), of which more later, if we are to establish the right kind of 'relationship' between the learner and the 'AI' computer teacher. But it leads to far more important and difficult issues concerning the nature of mind and whether the human mind can in fact be modelled by means of the computer.

In a real sense, much of the line of argumentation of Simons and others of his persuasion is not only empty speculation, but is entirely irrelevant to the actual state of the art of computing. If we are to come to an understanding of to what extent new ideas brought together, for the sake of convenience, under the umbrella of 'artificial intelligence', can be of relevance to CALL, it is essential to make as the starting point not some hypothetical future computing system, but the far less glamorous actual situation on the ground as it is now.

Without wishing to anticipate our consideration of algorithmic and non-algorithmic problem-solving techniques, it is important to record here that our infatuation with the machine goes far beyond simply admiring smoke-blackened engines 'shuffling gouts of steam', or the shiny cabinets of the large mainframe computing room with whirring tape decks and clattering line-printers.

It is all related to a conviction that somehow every problem is capable of being broken down into its component steps, or modularized, as we described earlier, and that since all machines to date have fitted into that pattern, there should be no reason to suspect that the computer is any different. AI should be capable of achievement by a process which ultimately will break the problem down into logical steps.

However, this notion is now very much open to challenge in the concepts of chaos and non-linearity which pose a considerable threat to that orthodoxy, and as Gleick points out, there is inevitable and considerable resistance to concepts which threaten to overturn a view of the world which is generally recognized and which enables 'established sciences to take for granted a body of knowledge that serves as a communal starting point for investigation' (Gleick, 1988, p. 39). If, however, you challenge the established notion of the logical decomposibility of problems, then there will be trouble. Here he is describing the reactions to the non-linear concepts of chaos and its reception by the scientific establishment, but the same holds true for views challenging the notion that AI can be attacked and conquered by anything but the conventional scientific techniques. Interestingly, he too is discussing an issue which crosses the boundaries between conventional disciplines:

> Work fell between disciplines — for example, too abstract for physicists yet too experimental for mathematicians. To some the difficulty of communicating the new ideas and the ferocious resistance from traditional quarters showed how revolutionary the new science was. Shallow ideas can be assimilated; ideas that require people to reorganize their picture of the world provoke hostility. (Gleick, 1988, p. 38.)

So the mechanistic model seems to fall down in more than one respect, and with it the enthusiasm of AI optimists appears to be on shaky ground, unless some new model emerges to replace the existing one. As yet, there is little sign of what that might be.

3.4   AI PESSIMISTS

The immediate problem for the non-expert who wishes to come to an understanding of the present state of AI is to determine precisely how to unscramble the speculative writing from the actual achievements of AI on the ground. One writer will claim, for example, that the expert system MYCIN 'has already out-performed human diagnosticians in the identification and treatment of blood infections and meningitis' (Simons, 1983, p. 58), whilst a more cautious (realistic?) view confesses that MYCIN is no more than a highly experimental and limited system which has as yet not been given a white coat and stethoscope and allowed to assume the role of a human intern. MYCIN faces serious problems of adaptation, both to non-standard input and also to complex disease interactions, and additionally has no real 'knowledge of the underlying physiological mechanisms whereby a disease process causes its manifestation'. (Knipers, 1987.)

Partridge may be writing tongue in cheek when he heads a chapter of his recent book on AI with these words: 'Half of what you hear about AI is not true; the other half is not possible'. (Partridge, 1986, p. 13.) But his wry comment does have the ring of truth about it. Speculation about AI is rife, but none of it is particularly helpful if you are attempting either to determine what has actually been achieved to date, or how to solve real problems in a live situation. Our fascination with the machine and in particular with fashioning machines in our own image has clouded over the practical issue of confronting the similarities and differences between man and computer as they exist now, drawing the appropriate conclusions and seeking to build upon that practical starting point. Sloman is perfectly right in his words of restraint to the over-enthusiastic pursuer of the intelligent machine:

> Instead of fruitless attempts to divide the world into things with and things without the essence of mind, or consciousness, we should examine the many detailed similarities and differences between systems. (Sloman, 1984, p. 42.)

He also rightly points out that, before we become carried away with the desire to create such machines, we really need to 'achieve a deeper understanding of the nature of our own minds' (p. 42). What Simons and others conveniently overlook or choose to disregard is the fact that we are very far from an understanding of the way in which the human mind works, and there is no purpose in injecting so-called intelligence into a computer until we have determined in some measure at least the way in which the human mind inputs and processes external sensory stimuli. Even if we treat the mind as a 'black box', the difficulties of simulating what happens between an input and an output from the black box are enormous.

But if we do not first succeed in making some sense of how the mind functions, we should simply be trying to implant into a machine something of which we have only a very imperfect knowledge, with all the attendant dangers that playing with fire bring in its train.

There is in such views as those of Simons no sense of a barrier — let alone a series of barriers — along the way, one or more of which might actually be insurmountable because of the different modalities of man and machine. The critics of AI are dismissed in the same terms as the alarmists who claimed that being transported at speed by the steam engine would cause injury and death to the human brain, or those who forced the early motor cars to be preceded by a man carrying a red flag, hardly a revolutionary banner ushering in a new age of mobile consumerism.

It has occurred to me as a mere humanist more than once that those who seek to turn machines into men are, at this very early stage of AI at least, wholly missing the point. Machines have certain qualities and limitations, and those are quite different from the qualities and limitations of human beings, and to seek to turn the one into the other involves attacking the limitations of the machine rather than building upon its strengths. Attempting a convergence of man and machine may, for the foreseeable future at least, be an entirely quixotic exercise, an academic self-indulgence which, given the powers of the forces with which we are dealing, can lead us into very dangerous waters indeed.

Dreyfus, in his book *What computers can't do*, explores what he perceives as the limits of what the computer can achieve, and the subtitle of the book *'A critique of artificial reason'* leaves the reader in no doubt as to his stance.

Dreyfus expresses the way in which the computing optimists put their case in these terms:

> If reason can be programmed into a computer, this will confirm an understanding of the nature of man which Western thinkers have been groping towards for two thousand years but which they only now have the tools to express and implement. (Dreyfus, 1972, p. 27.)

In other words, the theory is that the missing link in coming to a complete understanding of the human mind and making a working model of it has nothing to do with our own powers of insight or lack of them, but simply with the absence of the appropriate technology.

Dreyfus quotes the delightful phrase which Bar-Hillel concocted to explain this situation. He branded the phenomenon the 'fallacy of the successful first step'.

In other words, the temptation was to believe that because the first part of the problem resolved itself without too much effort the rest would be easy, and if it did not turn out to be easy, then the fault simply lay with the kind of techniques being used. Dreyfus repeats the words of another researcher, Vincent Guiliano, who worked in the field of automatic pattern recognition:

> Alas! I feel that many of the hoped-for objectives may well be porcelain eggs; they will never hatch, no matter how long heat is applied to them, because they require pattern discovery purely on the part of *machines* working alone. The tasks of discovery demand human qualities. (Dreyfus, 1972, p. 45.)

The argument is now that the technology in its earlier phases was not potent enough to crack the riddle of the way in which the human mind functions; now, however, with the coming of the transputer and the fifth generation of computers, all will be resolved.

Even though Dreyfus's book dates back to 1972, his critique is still powerful, and many of his assertions remain unchallenged. Although he wrote before the days of the transputer and the power that parallel processing has brought, his assertion that the information-processing model of mind is untenable still holds good:

> The answer to the question whether man can make such a machine must rest on the evidence of work being done. And on the basis of actual achievements and current stagnation, the most plausible answer seems to be, No. It is impossible to process an indifferent 'input' without distinguishing between relevant and irrelevant, significant and insignificant data.... If there is no promising empirical evidence, the whole self-supporting argument tumbles down like a house of cards. (Dreyfus, 1972, p. 99.)

The core of Dreyfus's argument, though, is what he regards as an extremely worrying trend in computer science. Nowhere else in scientific investigation has caution been so evidently thrown to the winds as in the predictions of the coming AI revolution:

> The need for a critique of artificial reason is a special case of a general need for critical caution in the behavioural sciences.... Experts have the responsibility of making clear the actual limits of their understanding and of the results they have so far achieved. A careful analysis of these limits will demonstrate that in virtually every domain of the social and behavioural sciences the results achieved to date will not support such 'extrapolation'.... Artificial

intelligence, at first glance, seems to be a happy exception to this pessimistic principle. (Dreyfus, 1972, p. xxvii.)

The central part of that passage is a direct quotation from Chomsky's *Language and Mind,* and parallels Bar-Hillel's fallacy of the first successful step. And for those who may be thinking that Dreyfus might well have been right in 1972, but that progress has been made since that time which renders such pessimism outdated, I quote from a recent review by Sutherland in the *Times Higher Educational Supplement* of a recent book by the same Minsky whom Dreyfus was castigating nearly two decades ago.

In *The society of mind*, Minsky is proposing that the mind is constituted of hierarchically arranged 'agents', a concept which is itself a hundred years old. Sutherland reacts in these words:

> Artificial intelligence is in danger of becoming the science of rediscovering well-known psychological concepts and giving them grandiose names.... Unfortunately Minsky does not get down to the task of specifying the exact interaction between the agents nor even how individual agents work.... He is more interested in a general outline of the mind than in its detailed workings, but this makes it virtually impossible to evaluate his ideas. (Sutherland, 1987, p. 17.)

Unsupported assertion based on a mechanistic view of man has created nothing but disappointment, and another cycle of assertions and hopes. Dreyfus's conclusion to his book is just as valid now as it was in 1972:

> If, however, one is willing to accept empirical evidence as to whether an effort has been misdirected, he has only to look at the predictions and the results. Even if there had been no predictions, only hopes, as in language translation, the results are sufficiently disappointing to be self-incriminating. (Dreyfus, 1972, p. 217.)

There is more than a little doubt as to the possibility of our being capable of creating a model of the human mind at all. We shall consider later the issues involved in formulating problems, the level of representation, the difficulties in organizing knowledge, and the different kinds of knowledge (knowledge about things and knowledge of how to do things) which are all prerequisites in the pursuit of AI programming, but it is useful to pause at this stage and consider briefly the wider issue of our knowledge of the human mind and how, and to what extent, that knowledge can be translated into programmable terms, whether in the traditional Von Neumann mode or in some kind of parallel-processing situation.

Weizenbaum takes the argument a stage further, by asserting that machines and men are so radically different that computers can never be turned into artificial men:

> And there precisely is the crucial difference between man and machine: Man, in order to become whole, must be forever an explorer of both his inner and his outer realities. His life is full of risks, but risks he has the courage to accept, because, like the

explorer, he learns to trust his own capacities to endure, to overcome. What could it mean to speak of risk, courage, trust, endur-
ance, and overcoming when one speaks of machines? (Weizenbaum, 1985, p. 280.)

3.5   DIFFERENCES BETWEEN MAN AND MACHINE

The first point which needs to be stressed, particularly for those unfamiliar
with the concepts and techniques of computer programming, is that it can be
extraordinarily difficult, if not impossible, to program a computer to
perform tasks which we, as humans, would regard as ridiculously simple. It
is important to understand why this is so.

Let us take, for example, an English sentence: 'The man gives a bone to
the dog'. That is a correct formulation on two levels. First, it is syntactically
correct; that is, there are no mistakes of grammar in the sentence. 'The man
give a bones to the dog' is not, and it would not be too demanding a task to
write a program which could unscramble such declarative utterances and
determine which are, or are not, correct.

The real difficulty arises when considering the second aspect of the
sentence's correctness. The logic of the sentence falls apart if we switch the
substantives around: 'A bone gives the dog to the man'. No human being
would make that kind of elementary error, since we all *know* that bones are
inanimate objects, incapable of acts of volition such as giving.

So we are back in that messy territory of weak algorithms, vast slabs of
half-digested world knowledge, non-deterministic, context-sensitive, self-
modifying programs, adequacy rather than accuracy — all those features, in
effect, which make AI such an intractable problem for the computer as we
know it.

The debate about the nature of intelligence and the existence of mind is
the first issue which demands clarification if we are to understand what areas
of AI can be applied to CALL.

3.6   THE CREDIBILITY GAP

There are two areas of AI which give rise to particular concern in the
informed outsider anxious to make sense of a complex situation. The first
concerns the gap between theory and practice, to which I alluded earlier in
the context of fudging over difficulties by pretending that they either do not
exist or that they can be readily resolved at some future (but as yet not
determined) date.

Such papering over the cracks is all too familiar in the literature, and I
will not burden the reader with a string of examples. Suffice it to say that
many such exercises are carried out with a degree of conviction which makes
it difficult for the non-initiate to determine whether the assertion is supported by experimental or other evidence, or whether it is a mere hope

masquerading as an actuality. So the outsider looking in on AI finds all manner of problems confronting an attempt to come to a clear understanding of the state of the art and the true capabilities of actual programs and practical concept.

3.7   THE AI PRAGMATISTS

Somewhere in between the two extremes of the pessimists and the optimists are to be found the AI pragmatists, who neither embrace the view that the computer is about to take over the world for good or ill, nor think that AI is dreaming the impossible dream. I tend towards the cautious view that:

> We are not machines, and machines are not people. Not now, and not for a long time to come. Personally, I think not ever, although at the far reaches of imagination this becomes an issue of philosophy. But as a practical, immediate consideration, no philosophical issue is involved. People are people. Machines are machines. Only a fool confuses them. (Crichton, 1984, p. 89.)

One of the factors which has caused the confusion is, I am sure, the publicity given to chess-playing programs and similar computer performances. Chess is regarded with awe as the ultimate intellectual human achievement, more a philosophical exploration of multidimensional complexities than a mere game. In fact, playing chess does not require as much raw 'intelligence' in terms of power or of different kinds of mental processing as many other areas of human activity. Chess is a closed domain, with no unpredictability (the rules are never changed in mid-game), nor does it require access to a vast knowledge base riddled with half-facts and ambiguities, in contrast to a real hard AI problem domain like computer speech recognition.

It requires less specifically 'human'-type intelligence to play chess than it does to perform daily routine acts which we regard as ridiculously simple, like opening the door of the refrigerator, removing an egg, lifting it without crushing it, and delicately cracking it on the edge of the frying pan.

That requires huge computing power, constant interaction and feedback through a number of input and output ports, including a three-dimensional vision capability. Chess, on the other hand, is a 'formal system', which is entirely self-contained, and shares with other formal systems the qualities of being digital and 'independent of the medium in which they are embodied'. (Haugeland, 1985, p. 58.) In addition, such systems are finite and based on a series of primitive operations which can be formulated into algorithms. Hence chess, given an appropriate level of computing power and programming skill, is neither an AI problem nor does it present any intractable insoluble difficulties to the programmer.

From a pragmatic point of view, the issue of power is of considerable importance. In the case of a chess program, it does not matter if the program takes several minutes to work out its next move, but in the case of a medical expert system, for example, 'even the most accurate of diagnoses slowly arrived at may not be useful, for instance, if in the meantime the patient dies' (Hayes *et al.*, 1983, p. 42). Nor would a computer vision system built into a car be of much value if it took minutes rather than fractions of a second to determine that the red glowing object in the line of sight is not the setting sun, but a red traffic light. Speedy response times are, of course, crucial in CALL.

My suspicion is that, as technology progresses apace, the computer will be able to simulate more intelligence with CD-ROM and similar technologies with access to huge knowledge bases. But the problems of access and interpretation remain stubbornly with us, as does the ultimate question as to whether intelligence is, after all, no more than a vast amount of processing power pushing back unintelligence to the point at which we no longer realize that the system is unintelligent.

The question of the essential nature of man and machine posed by Weizenbaum in the passage I cited earlier remains, in my mind, unanswered and unanswerable.

4

The human–computer interface

4.1 INTRODUCTION

So far, we have explored the past and present of CALL, and we have examined the complex question of the identity and general potentiality of AI. The next issue that must be considered is the nature of the interaction between man and machine and the expectations that each should have about the other. Human beings interact with other human beings, pet owners interact with their dogs, and misers interact with their hoarded gold. To humanists, and to language teachers in particular, though, it seems faintly ridiculous that humans can be said to have a 'relationship' of any kind with an electronic artefact like a computer. Surely this is another case of scientists in general and psychologists in particular exceeding the bounds of common-sense in the pursuit of arcane objectives.

At first sight, then, this chapter may be regarded as something of a diversion from our main purpose, but the human–computer interface is not only a key issue in its own right, but also needs to be thoroughly understood if we are to optimize the interaction between language learner and computer, particularly if we are seeking to venture into the much more difficult terrain of AI CALL. There will also be some spin-off benefit in examining this topic in that, by revealing some of the aspects of the way in which the novice and expert user approach the computer, it offers a first insight into the question of expert systems and their applicability to CALL, which we shall be examining in depth in a later chapter.

Even on the simplest level, it is crucial that the interaction between learner and computer should be as smooth and efficient as possible. Consider the following not unfamiliar scenario. The learner is told in certain circumstances to type Escape. He proceeds to do so, as he thinks, by typing in the letters E-S-C-A-P-E, and then wonders why either nothing happens or the computer's loudspeaker bleeps irritably at him. If you accept that such misunderstandings should be minimized or, better still, done away with altogether, you are well on the way to recognizing that the relationship between learner and machine is a very important constituent element indeed in CALL programming. In fact, this acceptance is a precondition for the creation of a successful working relationship between the two.

The way in which language learners interact with the computer is regrettably one of the most neglected aspects of CALL, but one which is so important that it must find a place in any discussion of the fundamentals of this field. In addition, the quality of the learning environment in which CALL takes place is of key contributory significance in all its aspects, even down to apparently unimportant considerations such as the colour of the walls, the lighting level, and even the physical appearance of the equipment itself. To this should be added the more complex ergonomic issues of the means by which the learner communicates with the computer, the manner in which the computer is programmed to respond to the learner, and the nature of the interaction between the two. If this is significant at the level of first-generation CALL, it is even more important when it comes to seeking to implement a higher, 'intelligent' form of language teaching on the computer.

It is all too easy to be dismissive of what appear at first sight to be fairly trivial issues, such as lighting or noise levels, but as the standard course book on the whole question of ergonomics in a working environment underlines (Oborne, 1987), there is a continuum of significance between the physical and human aspects of the situation and its potential to benefit or impact negatively on the working (in our case, learning) productivity of the people in that situation:

> Many hundreds of examples could be given to illustrate the fact that the quality of information transmitted from the operator to the system and back again is mediated by the environment. For this reason, the emphasis of modern ergonomics has been to investigate the operator and the environment as equal partners within the total working system, rather than to examine in minute detail the components which constitute any one man–machine loop. Ergono-mics, therefore seeks to consider ... the *total* interaction between the operator and the environment. (Oborne, 1987, p. 8.)

For operator, read learner, and for environment, read CALL learning situation.

The physical factors are indeed important, and not only because of the growing concern being expressed at the potential health hazards from screen radiation and other aspects of VDU (visual display unit) operation in particular. Governments, unions and employers in the Scandinavian countries have already taken such concerns seriously and have drawn up codes of practice for those who work with such equipment. However, this is not the appropriate place to consider in technical detail such matters as seating positions, screen position and flicker, and lighting, although they should be very much borne in mind in relation to CALL as in any other kind of learning environment. For a full account of their role, see Oborne (1985, 1987).

The non-pedagogical aspects of the location where CALL work is to take place are of considerable significance because of their potential to promote or impede its overall capability as a teaching medium. And the 'total interaction' on which Oborne rightly places so much emphasis also includes in my view what kind of name is given to the physical environment. Even if an identical set of activities takes place within the same set of four walls, changing the title of the location from 'classroom', say, to 'lecture theatre' immediately shifts the level and nature of the expectations of those about to enter and be taught, and thus their attitude to the activities undergoes a more or less significant change.

What concerns me considerably in this respect is the re-emergence or straight adaptation of the unfortunate term 'laboratory' in relation to CALL. I am at a loss to offer a more appropriate name, but I have never been happy either with the pseudo-scientific overtones implied by the term 'language laboratory', nor by the kind of environment which the language laboratory has created and which has been inherited by what is now almost universally entitled the 'CALL laboratory'.

I find inappropriate the notion of a 'laboratory' situation for learning a language, whether that be the conventional language laboratory or the CALL laboratory, since it imparts the wrong kind of signals to the learner. It implies both an inappropriate kind and level of interaction between learner and environment, in the way in which the technology is presented to the learner, both in terms of the physical equipment itself and — most importantly of all — in the nature of the interaction between learner and computer.

In what follows, the emphasis is on the language laboratory, because it is the technological precursor of CALL and it points to the directions in which it is desirable for CALL to be channelled.

4.2   THE PHYSICAL ENVIRONMENT

The design and layout of technological environments for language learning, mostly in the form of language laboratories, has, in my estimation, impacted negatively on their potential as productive learning environments. The two principal design philosophies for language laboratories have been equally deficient in this regard, although, to be fair, the furniture design has been severely constrained by the technological limitations of the equipment. Those layouts are either that consisting of serried ranks of booths all facing the front, with the teacher in turn facing the class at the — usually raised — control console in a mechanized parody of the traditional classroom format, or the approach in which the booths line the walls and the learners face the wall to work with the equipment, then swing round to face the teacher when the time comes to work away from the technology.

In both cases, operating with headphones, isolated, apart from the occasional intervention of the teacher's voice, and with little or no visual stimulation or reinforcement to the learning situation, is hardly designed to promote the creation of an enjoyable, productive and appropriate learning situation unless the learners are very strongly motivated indeed. In addition, the artificial and machine-dominated nature of the environment tends to distance the learner from the realities of acquiring foreign language skills. I suspect, in fact, that the physical aspects of the language laboratory even more than any pedagogical deficiencies in the teaching material have contributed significantly to its falling into disfavour.

Many of the drawbacks of the language laboratory have been attributable to deficiencies in the hardware available for the given technology, with uncomfortable seating positions caused by the depth necessary in the desk to accommodate a reel-to-reel recorder, too much of the desk top taken over by equipment to permit note pads and course books to be accommodated, and, until recently, the need for side panels to act as sound barriers between the individual booths. The most up-to-date equipment such as the Tandberg IS10 is now sufficiently unobtrusive to allow acceptable desk space, a good sitting position, and headphones of such efficient sound buffering quality that an open plan seating arrangement is possible, without the need for side panels, which in the past have served further to isolate the learner from the rest of the learning environment.

Given all its drawbacks, the original 'modern' shine of the language laboratory with its aura of brisk, efficient new methodologies rather than the somewhat amateurish muddle and rigidly grammatical approach of the past soon began to wear off as language teachers began to recognize that a teaching situation in which technology replaces human–human interaction must have clear and demonstrable advantages, even in limited areas of language teaching, if their use is to be justified by the teacher and accepted by the user.

Teachers increasingly came to ask themselves a simple question: is the language laboratory, with all its defects and rigidities, offering a better and more productive learning environment than the classroom, with all the problems inherent in that mode of seeking to involve the entire group of learners in furthering their productive skills? It seemed in the early stages of the language laboratory's development that the answer was in the affirmative, not least because it allowed a whole class to be practising productive skills in a way in which it is not possible in a conventional classroom situation. However, there is a world of difference between producing an (albeit infrequent) utterance in a foreign language with instant corrective feedback on the part of the teacher, and merrily reinforcing incorrect pronunciation and other errors for the length of a whole session if the unfortunate learner does not happen to be monitored by the teacher at the instant at which the error first makes itself manifest.

Now, however, the situation at best is that the jury is, so to speak, still out on that matter, and many language teachers have given their verdict against the language laboratory, in non-intensive teaching contexts at least. It has always seemed odd to me, to put it at its mildest, that a living thing like the spoken language, which depends critically on social interaction for its proper context, should so readily have been transported into a synthetic environment totally unlike its natural surroundings which has been made to play such a major role in the learning process.

In the first two generations of language laboratories — the reel-to-reel systems and the first cassette-based laboratories — the bulk of the equipment, the ducted wiring, and other factors also necessitated its permanent location in a room exclusively set aside for the purpose. The latest generation of equipment does, as I have indicated, at least hold out the possibility of a far more flexible approach to the location (and indeed the application) of the equipment. This means that the idea of a class or group of students having to be timetabled for an hour marked in advance 'language laboratory practice' can now potentially yield place to a far more flexible approach to the technology which will enable it to be employed at times when it fits appropriately into the teaching pattern rather than having to be engineered into a fixed weekly hour.

4.3   A 'REAL' ENVIRONMENT FOR CALL

4.3.1   A poor substitute

At best, the language laboratory makes a poor substitute for an interaction with a human teacher, and for this reason alone its applicability is limited, except in specialized situations where highly motivated adults are being trained intensively to speak or interpret. Clearly, too, it can have an important role for *ab initio* learners. Using a laboratory in normal teaching situations can, however, be rather like teaching a pilot how to fly an unfamiliar aircraft by means of pencil and paper exercises, instead of in a simulator which offers at least a reasonable approximation of the 'real' situation. This situation has, to some extent, been alleviated in the past by the use of overhead projector (OHP) slides or still or cine projection, and now the possibility of IV or CDI coupled with a computer does hold the promise of a less artificial learning environment, and, more importantly, one at least slightly less distant from the actual situations in which human language is normally used.

I have dwelt at some length on the language laboratory and its problems since they are not dissimilar to those facing anyone designing a learning environment for CALL. My concern is that a similar fate of remoteness from reality and an inappropriately technological 'feel' should not befall the room set aside for CALL learning, nor degrade the nature of the experience which the CALL learner acquires. It is unfortunate, but almost inevitable, that such rooms should be designated 'CALL laboratories', particularly since, while a collection of tape recorders with headsets all linked to a master console may not be perceived as particularly scientific, a microcomputer certainly is regarded as a product of science which is dedicated to scientific activities.

4.3.2   The term 'laboratory'

Let us consider the word 'laboratory' and its implications in more detail. To be cynical for a moment, the term itself might help a hard-pressed humanities faculty to capture funding within a highly competitive bidding system in an educational institution, in which scientific colleagues can conceive of the purpose and fundamentals of a language laboratory. However, I am satisfied — although I cannot produce hard evidence to support my assertion — that the use of the term 'laboratory' has itself contributed to an inappropriate attitude to such learning environments on the part of both learner and teacher. The word implies not only a certain kind of white-coated physical environment, but also a situation in which investigations are undertaken abstracted from the real world outside, *in vitro* rather than *in vivo*, so to speak. The activities which take place in a language 'laboratory' are, however, in substance and intent quite different from those for which a scientific laboratory has been designed.

Language learners are not conducting experiments with the materials with which they operate: the tasks undertaken in the language laboratory are synthetic rather than analytic in function. The learner is not taking something apart to find out what makes it function, but is rather trying to employ the building bricks of language in the construction of speech acts, using transformational techniques where appropriate:

> Language acquisition ... is a process in which the learner actively goes about trying to organise his perceptions of the world in terms of linguistic concepts. (Diller, 1978, p. 58.)

But, whether or not you find the analogy satisfactory from that point of view, it seems to me to fall down crucially in two other respects. The first relates to the notion of learning language to aspire towards being a 'scientific' activity, the second concerns the nature of the equipment itself.

Many of the swings of fashion in language learning can be attributed to the fact that language teachers are uncomfortable with the reality that learning a modern language always tends to be a messy and uncoordinated business which needs structuring in some way or other in order to be able to permit the learner to advance through the learning process in a structured and cumulative manner. 'Easy' material has to be learned before 'difficult' material. Equally, the standard rules in a given situation have to be acquired before the irregularities can be learned.

The present tense comes before the pluperfect subjunctive, straighforward declarative utterances before impossible conditions in past time, verbs followed by the accusative case before those taking the genitive or dative. New methodologies typically display a desire either to impose some form of order and discipline on to this somewhat chaotic situation, or claim to detect a hidden order beneath the disorder; taking their cue from either of these premises, they construct an approach to language teaching which claims to offer a rational and ordered solution to the problem of how to teach a foreign language successfully.

Unfortunately, as all attempts to design all-embracing grammars and exclusive approaches have demonstrated, language as a human activity refuses to fit neatly into any scientific constraints. General principles and specific rule subsets can be drawn out and demonstrated, but there is always an exception to the rule, an element of nonlinearity (to borrow a current scientific term) which refuses to permit the phenomenon of human language to fall like a jigsaw neatly into place and to behave in a stable and predictable fashion. It is particularly important, then, when using mechanical means to teach language, to recognize this fact, and not to give the learner the entirely false impression that language is a scientifically transparent phenomenon, not least because the learner, as he advances from being a novice to a competent speaker, will himself recognize the fact and see through the deception.

In addition, the learner should not be deceived into regarding the acquisition of language skills as a reductionist activity, in which it is possible to home in on individual areas and build up a skill profile by mastering these areas in isolation. Language learning is not a process of breaking down and simplifying; on the contrary, it is all about mastering and accepting ever-increasing complexities.

The more significant concern, though, relates to the technology in the learning situation. In the language laboratory, this is important enough, but it is even more so when the power of the computer is introduced, particularly if we are to seek to apply that computer in more than the 'unintelligent' mode of first-generation CALL.

If the computer is to play a role in language learning at all, it should be perceived by the learner as offering an environment for learning which is relevant to his needs and appropriate to learning a language rather than conducting, say, an experiment in physics or biochemistry.

4.3.3 Physical layout

When it comes to the CALL physical environment, I must confess that I have found most of the early CALL learning situations, those in my own department included, to be rather depressing locations, with amateurish-looking machinery untidily laid out and of a less than welcoming appearance. The first generation of micros certainly did little to present a professional appearance to the learning situation, with separately purchased keyboards, visual display units, and disk drives, all of different designs and finishings, and linked by a tangle of wires. The quality of many of the visual displays again did not encourage concentrated learning, being mostly composite video signals, in which the colour in particular was of indifferent quality.

Now, however, one-plug microcomputers in three — or, in some cases, two — boxes enclose screen, processors, disk drives and keyboard in much more professional casings, largely due to pressure from the potential business market.

In the physical environment, care should be taken to ensure that the arrangement of computers and seating does not imply a one-to-one relationship between learner and computer. In the language laboratory, the beginnings of learner–learner interaction can be seen in the 'pairing' features which permit fixed — or even random — pairs of learners to communicate directly with each other. In the case of the computer, it has been recognized that group interaction with the screen display means that the business of drilling or improving inferencing ability need be no longer a matter of isolated drudgery, but of group discussion and interaction. In fact, it offers the prospect of efficient and 'safe' learner-directed education through the medium of CALL without the necessity for teacher intervention.

In addition, working with CALL tends to be on the basis of individuals and groups going at their own pace with different material, rather than of a classroom-type coordinated learning process, so from this point of view too the layout can be far less formal.

4.3.4 Screen considerations

But that is not the end of the story. There are aspects of even the most up-to-date microcomputing equipment which render it problematical as a teaching tool. These include the screen size and 'landscape' format, which is not particularly well suited to the reading and editing of continuous text, and the keyboard which requires a certain modicum of skill. Various alternatives have been proposed but none has penetrated the market place to any extent, except for specialized applications, notably desktop publishing (DTP).

Screen glare, sitting positions, and so forth, are unglamorous topics which we have already touched on, but they do impact substantially on the learner.

There are also other ergonomic problems to be considered in the design of screen layout. When I first discovered flashing purple on a yellow background my more psychedelic colours became a departmental standing joke, but I soon learned both to tone the colours down, and to ensure that legibility was fostered and eyestrain minimized.

An equally important consideration is the use of colour coding as an adjunct to learning. It is not simply a matter of ensuring legibility, though: colour coding, if consistent and wisely chosen, can both act as a positive aid to learning and even encourage the appropriate mental states conducive to effective learning.

A consistent application of the same colour mix for the same set of operations assists the user considerably in overcoming any familiarization difficulties, particularly in relation to activities secondary to the actual learning process, such as listing the files available on the disk, choosing and loading the appropriate exercise, and so forth.

As for the screen itself, modern medium to high resolution colour displays offer a reasonable quality of definition and lack of blurred and unstable images so characteristic of composite video signals on standard TV screens. Of course, the designer should be aware of deficiencies within a given range of options, such as the less than adequate definition of a CGA text screen within the IBM PC range of options. In such cases, intense foreground colour can overcome the somewhat spindly text that otherwise appears on screen.

Legibility of text and other such practical matters are clearly of importance. It does not require a detailed knowledge of factors such as research results which, not surprisingly, point to the fact that 'the maximum error rates occurred when the character and background colours had wavelengths close to each other (for example, violet on blue, yellow on green)'. (Oborne, 1987, p. 128.) A commonsense application of yellow on a dark ground produces the most restful results, and it is consoling to see that it matches the research investigations into this area (Radl, quoted by Oborne, 1987, p. 127).

There has been a considerable amount of research into the relative ease with which material can be read and understood from the screen or from paper, and the results appear to come out to the disadvantage of the former:

> By far the most common experimental finding is that reading from screen is significantly slower than reading from paper. (Dillon *et al.*, 1988, p. 457.)

The results, it seems, indicate a 20–30% lower speed of reading, coupled with a poorer accuracy for proof-reading activities. Dillon's survey (1988) of the literature indicates that the results are far from clear-cut, however, and that there does not seem to be any one undisputed cause of lower performance rates in reading from the screen as opposed to reading from paper, apart, that is, for the fairly obvious (but now mercifully infrequent) problems caused by inferior screen image quality:

> Although reading from computer screens may be slower and sometimes less accurate than reading from paper, no one variable is likely to be responsible for this difference. (Dillon *et al.*, 1988, p. 463.)

Another important consideration is the amount of information presented on the screen at any one time. It is vital to avoid cluttering the screen with an excess of sensory inputs, since this can obviously rapidly become counterproductive. A simple, clean appearance to the screen with the main information clearly highlighted is an essential prerequisite for good-quality CALL.

The location of the information is also of significance, particularly as an adjunct to colour coding. If help information is always available by pressing a certain function key option highlighted on a menu bar at the bottom of the screen in a given mix of colours, that is a further element of support to the user.

All these factors, however unimportant they may seem to be at first acquaintance, are essential contributory factors in the establishment and maintenance of a consistent and positive relationship between learner and computer.

4.3.5 Artificial learning

The tide of enthusiasm for the application of these technologies to language learning has in recent years begun to be challenged by a growing chorus of voices of caution, which have warned on ergonomic grounds against an over-enthusiastic application of computing technology in particular. Much of this caution has paralleled my own concern about the use of the term 'laboratory'.

The concerns focus on the artificiality of the learning environment, and I mention them here because we have been considering this aspect so far on a practical rather than abstract level. It is now being argued in some circles that unthinking acceptance of a key role of the computer in learning situations, despite the apparent success that it enjoys, contains real dangers which must be brought to the surface and debated openly. The implied assumption that the computer means progress, and that progress is inevitably a good thing, has come under strong challenge.

Concerns have been expressed that, not just in language learning, the computer has been applied inappropriately in learning situations, particularly among the younger primary school learners where real concrete situations offer both a stronger impact and a more tangible basis for further development than the superficial attractions of a flickering two-dimensional image on a computer screen. In addition, there is the danger that the computer does not foster the growth of imagery and the imagination, but offers a perspective of reality that is 'basically mechanistic':

> Modern education often seems ... to have lost all sense of the cognitive significance of the feeling–emotional life. (Sloan, 1984b, p. 4.)

It is argued further that the computer offers, not a parallel to, but an impoverishment of the quality of experience which real life situations present:

> The added dimension of interaction with the screen is small compensation when one thinks of the usual large-muscle, full-bodied movements characteristic of young children as they interact directly with the environment. ... There is an absence of texture, of smell, a lessening of qualitative associations with the experience of painting. (Cuffaro, 1984, p. 24.)

The context of the quotation is that of the computer art class versus the traditional art class. Davy, in the same collection of papers, is even more vehement:

> The actual learning environment is almost autistic in quality, impoverished sensually, emotionally, and socially. (Davy, 1984, p. 12.)

Autism is a condition in which the patient can get on to good terms with objects, but finds it difficult to relate to other people.

Of course, CALL typically is dealing with a maturer age group of learners, but we should always be conscious of the dangers that the human–computer interface can present. It can all too readily offer a scientific model of the world in which facts swamp the imaginative powers; it does not allow for the full participation of the senses in the way in which other learning situations can; and, finally, it can tend to offer a false sense of security to those who find interpersonal relations challenging, and seek the solace of interacting with a mindless machine.

So from the point of view of selecting appropriate and non-trivial contexts for the application of CALL, the learning environment should also be carefully considered, since it in no way offers a full-blooded surrogate for real language-based communication between people. We must always remain conscious of these severe limitations of the computer, even in our most enthusiastic moments of support for CALL. The wisest words of such caution I have found come in the faint praise with which Sloan damns the computer as an educational tool:

> The computer, like the automobile, it is suggested, may entail some casualties but it will greatly enhance convenience, comfort, and the possibilities for personal communication among the majority of its users. (Sloan, 1984b, p. 2.)

4.4   THE LEARNING ENVIRONMENT

Having considered the physical environment and its impact at various levels, I turn now to investigating the interaction between learner and computer from the point of view of the learning situation itself, and in so doing we examine one particular aspect of ergonomics (or human factors, as the Americans call it), the HCI.

The field of the human–computer interface or HCI used to be given the title MMI, or man–machine interface, and the shift to a different name does indeed underpin the fact that the nature of the relationship has changed dramatically. Unfortunately, a change in name has not brought with it a sharpening of focus in relation to the nature, role and functions of this area of investigation. A recent introduction to a series of articles on the HCI complains as follows:

> HCI probably has as many meanings as there are people engaged in it. (Damodaran, 1988, p. 385.)

That is a touch of legitimate hyperbole induced by a sense of confusion at the diverse different fields in which the HCI has been investigated, from detailed practical aspects to the structure of complex software environments. Our concern here is of necessity selective, and the areas which need to be investigated are, first, what might be termed the 'balance of power' between human and computer and how that has shifted over the years; second, the concept of the virtual machine; next, the modality of interaction between human and computer; and finally, and most importantly, criteria for best practice in the CALL situation.

First, though, a brief consideration of this word 'relationship' in the context of the HCI, which, to a language teacher may well seem more than a little inapposite when applied to a piece of computing equipment. This may to a computing outsider sound a little far-fetched, but it is just as important for a learner to understand what a computer is asking of him, and too for that learner to have confidence in the methodology and expertise of the program as it is in the case of a human tutor:

> It may be objected that there surely should be no problem at all, since 'seeing' or 'understanding' is normally so successful, and so effortless, that one of the hardest problems in first coming to study

psychology is to appreciate that there is anything to explain. (Allport, 1980, p. 48.)

Things which human beings do so readily and seemingly without effort, cannot be simply mapped onto any existing computer system, as a result of which there is a real challenge in designing an interface which offers a genuinely user-friendly interaction without making impossible demands on the computing system.

At the point of interface between the human being and the machine, therefore, there lies a whole range of complex and difficult issues that need to be understood and resolved if any kind of interaction is to succeed, and this is particularly significant in the case of CALL, where the learner is using the computer in order to achieve a pedagogical objective which has hitherto been arrived at either in interaction with passive objects such as books or tapes, or with other human beings, that is to say, the peer group of learners and the teacher.

4.5   THE BALANCE OF POWER

In the past (and to some extent, in the present too), it has been the case in the context of the HCI that human operators have to subordinate themselves to the convenience of the computer. The real heart of the problem, though, is not simply that computers tended to be designed exclusively for the expert programmer, nor that the programmer had to have a thorough conversance with the details of the functioning of those computers which the command structures available in modern operating systems more or less renders unnecessary. The problem runs deeper than that:

> Most methodologies give primary attention to the functions of the system being developed and the data upon which it operates. ... The user interface to the system is frequently only considered as an afterthought. For interactive systems, though, these approaches may not work well, since user-oriented considerations must receive attention very early in the development process. Furthermore, user concerns and user preferences must have priority over some system-oriented considerations. (Wasserman, 1985, p. 611.)

In other words, there is little point in a modern interactive system in designing it away from the end user. The user must be designed into the system from the beginning, since he is a crucial part of it. The user should not have to perform a kind of post facto designing job on himself, as it were, to re-engineer himself in order to fit in with the arbitrary parameters and working structures of a pre-designed package. So the term 'user-friendliness' means much more than a computer interface programmed to say please and thank you; it is a crucially important consideration in the total design of any interactive package.

The notion of user-friendliness is, surprisingly, quite a recent arrival on the computing scene, and in particular any reader who is a mainframe user will be all too familiar with the fact that they have to spend more man-hours wrestling with the idiosyncrasies of the operating system than with productive programming.

The human being had to adapt himself to the requirements of the computing machine, which were complex, rigid, and machine-centred. In addition, it was in the early years of computing most frequently the case that the human being never actually came into direct contact with the computer at all: the programming or data capture work was done off-line, with decks of punched cards or reels of tape handed in at reception, and hours later output returned in the form of line-printer paper or more paper tape.

So the question of 'live', on-line interaction simply did not arise, and even when the multiuser on-line systems became a reality, the user was in no way shielded from the complexities of the operating system, nor from the line-oriented modes of input and output. To this day, such primitive forms of interaction are still standard in many mainframe environments, and on some machines little seems to have changed since the 1960s, except for the fact that machine–machine communications now no longer involves sending magnetic tapes through the post — on- or off-line electronic communications are now a reality.

The most significant psychological impact on that mode of interaction between mainframe and terminal user which has carried over into the microcomputer environment, and one from which it is essential to shield the CALL user, is, in my view, that of the notion of 'rightness' and 'wrongness', and how that is conveyed to the user.

The least desirable aspect of such system design is that the responses to user interaction are regarded as either 'right' or 'wrong'. In other words, the concept of an 'error', of having infringed against one or more of a set of rules which may be perceived as arbitrary or impenetrable, or both, is central. At the very least, such an approach is not conducive to infusing the user with confidence, and at worst, the constant fear of being 'wrong' can seriously impede any progress the user wants to make in actually using the system at all:

> The efficient interaction between a person and the environment in which that person operates will occur only if the two are matched in requirements and abilities.... Just as it is necessary to ensure physical compatibility between the user and the computer system, so it is important that they are compatible at a cognitive level.... The machine's model of the user's behaviour needs to be compatible with the user's model of the machine's. (Oborne, 1985, p. 253.)

For reasons which will become clearer when we consider in more detail the differences between the novice and the expert, there is a world of difference in response and reaction between novice and expert when an error message appears on the screen.

Take for example the famous and notorious CP/M error message which greets you when you attempt to Pip a file to a medium on which there is no space: ERROR WRITE NO DATA BLOCK. To an expert, such a message holds no terrors, since he has a more or less complete overall picture of the situation within which he is operating. Even if the error message is unfamiliar to the expert, his reaction is conditioned by the fact that he has gained sufficient experience with the system to know how to set about trying to troubleshoot that particular problem.

The expert, in other words, has a model of the system with which he is interacting built up in his mind. He can evolve strategies for rectifying any failures in the interaction process by calling on that model and his experience of past situations.

The novice, on the other hand, has no such intellectual tools at his disposal, and one of a number of unfortunate and inappropriate reactions on his part will result in the situation remaining unresolved and the learner losing confidence in his own abilities and in the system with which he is operating.

In any interaction with the computer for an applications purpose, particularly when the user is naive, it is crucial that the 'noise-to-signal' ratio should be as favourable as possible, that the effectiveness of the interaction should be maximized, and that the user, naive or not, should not be provided with an unrequested lesson in how not to program the computer.

The past of HCI is, with some few laudable exceptions, littered with illustrations of what can best be described as a Calvinist view of man's relationship with the computer. In other words, the rules (I nearly typed 'commandments') appear to have been established by some stern and unforgiving deity, and failure to observe them in the minutest detail leads inevitably into a state of 'error', a sin of commission or omission rectifiable only by the user's retreating back a stage in order to try and redeem himself. Unfortunately, some 'errors', involving, for example, file erasure, tend to be beyond redemption.

To take a very straightforward example of the awfulness of an existing system: one on-line computerized library cataloguing system requires the user to type a three-character code (no more, no less), followed by pressing the SEND key. The code 'AUT', for example, summons up the routine which gives access to the author index. In the case of title searches, however, the system designers clearly felt that the sensitivities of lady librarians would be offended by applying the same convention to the first three letters of the word 'title', so the code is coyly modified to TIL, a far from untypical example of a system setting up inflexible parameters to the user interface, and then falling foul of its own restrictions.

It would have been far simpler to have introduced a number list of options which would involve the user in a single keystroke rather than four (or more, if the code is miskeyed). The reaction of the system to such miskeying is equally unhelpful. It baldly states that it does not recognize the command and requires the user to start again. It is, of course, far easier from the system programmer's point of view to devise an environment of this level of inflexibility: it is far more complicated and challenging to provide a kinder mode of interaction with context-sensitive help for the naive and advanced user alike.

Now the debate about the HCI has advanced beyond the level of how to minimize the 'user-hostility' or even 'user-indifference' of many systems. That is the case at least in the journal and conference literature — it is emphatically not so in the vast majority of operating systems currently available. Only where a package is designed to shield the user from the system in, for example, a WIMP environment (windows, icons, mice and pull-down menus) is the right kind of interactive background being established, but these are no more than tentative first advances along a very long road indeed.

It still seems almost heretical to voice a complaint such as one might legitimately in the mainframe environment I have been using for the past five years to the effect that the Simula programs I write, when run interactively, accept a straight file name for input or output purposes. Simula is really no more than a superset of Algol 60, so I find it incomprehensible that in similar interactions with the latter language, the system hangs if I forget to type in a file name with double quotes round it, as Algol demands, and when I break into the program an inscrutable error message is generated. It really does demand a revolution in the thinking of system designers to force them to write with the user, rather than the machine, in mind. The revolution has started in the micro environment, but it has yet to filter up to the mainframe systems-programming fraternity. It is equally incomprehensible to me why it is still necessary, when wishing to use a computing package, from SPSS to the OCP, to hack my way through a bulky manual riddled with rules and regulations apparently designed to place as many obstacles as possible between the potential user and the applications package he wishes to employ. One of the key contributions of the home computer explosion has been the fact that the majority of purchasers, such as those who require the Amstrad PCW range as a word processing engine, simply refuse to undergo such a long and arduous initiation process before actually being permitted the great privilege of using the system for the purpose for which they purchased it.

So it is important for a whole number of reasons that the 'balance of power' between user and computer should be properly adjusted, that the interaction should not be computer-centric, and that the interaction between human and computer should be one between equals, as it were, rather than in a context in which the human has to struggle to come to terms with complex and arbitrary-seeming rules which are designed to meet the convenience of the computing system, not the user.

However, user-friendliness is very much a matter of balance. If a system is overloaded with, say, obtrusive help facilities this may itself impede the efficiency of the interaction:

> Although help facilities may increase inexperienced users' performance, if they are unable to be halted they can slow down experienced users who do not need them; if the system is too 'friendly' it is likely to constrain the experienced user in its use. (Oborne, 1985, p. 250.)

This holds within it an important implication in the design of CALL software. One design assumption should be that the software must be capable of being productively used within moments of a complete computing novice sitting down at the keyboard. Those early moments in the interactive process are vital to the establishment of a proper basis for a dialogue between learner and computer and for the pedagogic efficiency of the interaction. But novices, after a halting start, rapidly develop into more practised users of the system. This was true even in the days of mainframe CALL, and it rapidly became evident that the level of support available to the first-time user should be capable of being gradually withdrawn on a sliding scale and under the control of the user himself if user-friendliness was not to become stifling and impact negatively on the interaction.

As we shall see, it is relatively easy to design a system which offers a high level of support to the beginner; it is equally straightforward to present a high-powered but more demanding interface to the expert; but what is a far from trivial exercise is to design a system which meets the needs of both, and of others at varying stages of expertise in between, without losing in speed, efficiency, or appropriateness in the level of help and support.

4.6   THE VIRTUAL MACHINE

And indeed it is becoming evident to the designers of computer systems and software that 'we will increasingly build systems top-down from user needs rather than bottom-up from technological availability'. (Gaines, 1985, p. 4.) Compare and contrast the mainframe line editors, and their descendants like Edlin in the MS-DOS environment, with their full screen successors like Locoscript and Wordstar and the newest generation of word processors. Edlin, for example, which is only a marginal improvement on the awful CP/M Ed program, is littered with anti-personnel devices which can erase whole lines of text with an inadvertent double keystroke or insert commands in the text if the user momentarily forgets which mode he is in. Such hostile interfaces are a world away from the current generation of editors with their spelling checkers, thesaurus facilities, and single-key commands.

In addition, the mode of interaction has shifted away from that of the single command line in which more or less impenetrable commands with parameter lists are laboriously keyed in (with all the error-proneness which this implies), to the concept of the windows environment, and a user interface of the level of sophistication such as one finds on the more advanced contemporary desktop microcomputers like the Amiga 2000, with its workbench interface which is a state of the art WIMP environment.

The analogy of the workbench with drawers containing projects — as opposed to disks containing subdirectories holding files — is far more supportive to the user than the traditional user interfaces, although it is not without its demerits.

Problems of user psychology should also not be underrated, particularly when dealing with naive, or first-time, users of the computer. In such situations it is a matter of prime importance that the user should certainly be aware of the fact that the computer is a piece of technology which will make quite different, and more challenging, demands than a programmable washing machine or videorecorder, but at the same time the modularities of man and machine must be brought as close together as is possible: 'It is [the novice's] reluctance (and inability) to passively accept the system *as it is* that causes most of the learning difficulty we have observed.' (Carroll, 1985, p. 40.) Carroll offers an illustration of the way in which the user both fails to treat the computer as a machine incapable of reacting in a human manner, and also assumes that he or she has somehow interacted incorrectly with the computer:

> One participant, who finally succeeded in executing an operation after more than one try, wondered whether her earlier failures were somehow due to her having hit the Enter key 'in the wrong way'. (Carroll, 1985, p. 39.)

HCI researchers consider the computer as a 'virtual machine' in any given interaction environment. In other words, a user at the level of a word processor or spreadsheet package sees the computer as a word processor or spreadsheet and nothing else. It is of no interest to the user whether the package is written in 8086 assembler or in BASIC, for that matter, nor what the operation system design constraints are, so long as the interaction achieves its objectives with the minimum of obstacles between user and machine. The test is simply whether the task which the user wishes to undertake is performed in a satisfactory and productive manner. This has fundamental implications for the AI-type interaction in CALL.

The next stage along the path, then, seems to be to design the HCI in such a way that the learner is scarcely aware of the fact that he is dealing with a computer at all.

4.7   THE MODALITY OF INTERACTION

To the outsider the objective of making the computer seem not to be a computer at all seems more than a little quixotic. When a human being interacts with another person or object, he adjusts the modality of the interaction according to that individual or object. The nature of that adjustment seems to me to be a positive rather than a negative input into the interaction, and the attempt to turn the computer into a real person prompts the question as to what kind of person, since there is no such thing as an abstract generalized human being.

The interaction between man and machine, whether that machine is a drinks dispenser or a Cray 2, is of necessity different from that between one human being and another, and desirably so. A user who elicits a non-human response after having been deluded into believing that he is dealing with a real voice at the other end of the telephone line will, at the very least, have his confidence in the interaction severely damaged. We hardly require learned papers to inform us that the interaction between human and human is of a different order from that between humans and machines.

Linguists will in particular find it strange that the computing fraternity appears not to have taken up the linguistic concept of 'register' and adapted and extended it into the context of the HCI. The HCI is in effect an extension of the notion of register into the man–machine context, in which certain conventions are followed which, if reasonably well formulated, are swiftly assimilated and accepted by the human user. Such sets of conventions are familiar to us in all aspects of our daily lives. This is so much the case that we may need reminding of the fact that, for example, we accept that in opera tenors who are stabbed to death appear capable of singing about their demise for a good quarter of an hour, and in cinema and television camera angles change in a manner which 'primitive' people unused to such media would find baffling until they had learned to accept and assimilate them.

It is not even certain that the ultimate objective of the HCI is for the human being and the computer to 'talk' to each other. Newell argues that the modalities of computer and human being are so different that it is wrong to assume that they can most usefully interact in the human modality of speech. He takes as an illustration the use of subtitles in television as an aid for viewers with a hearing handicap. The modalities of speech and the written word are quite different, so that 'it is rarely good enough just to reproduce the words which are being spoken'. (Newell, 1985, p. 233.) He goes on to argue that speech has actually got serious disadvantages when it comes to communicating with a machine. Speech is:

> '. . . very slow compared with direct controls such as keys and visual display . . . it is transitory . . . it cannot be scanned . . . it is more error prone . . . sometimes ambiguous.' (Newell, 1985, p. 235.)

In order that the learner can enjoy a beneficial relationship with the computer, then, it is necessary both to ensure that the modality of interaction is both appropriate to the circumstances and one which optimizes the learning process which is, after all, at the heart of the matter. In seeking to obtain this objective, it seems to me that pretending that the computer does not exist is a less than wise course. On the contrary, establishing a proper register with which to interact with the computer enables the learner to work within a set of parameters in which the conventions are clearly spelled out in advance, so that there is no worrying of 'how to behave', as it were, and the majority of effort can be concentrated on the learning process. And the set of conventions established should be one appropriate to the computer and not one which tries to pretend that the computer is something other.

4.8   OPTIMUM HCI PRACTICE FOR CALL

Let us assume, then, that we are dealing with a virtual machine, which still retains its identity as a computer to the user, typically consisting of a keyboard and screen (as far as the user is concerned). Nowadays, with the increasing availability of hard disks on microcomputers, even the autoboot-ing disk is becoming a thing of the past. The learner recognizes this equipment as a computer, but is not burdened, then, with the need for any pre-training or familiarization beyond the practicalities of ensuring that the machine is switched on and which way the disks, if used, are to be inserted in the drive.

4.8.1 Physical context
The first requirement is that the computing system should be of professional appearance and in a learning environment which does not exude an inappropriate atmosphere of laboratory-like paraphernalia, with trailing wires and test equipment scattered around. Office-type swivel chairs with good back support are also desirable, especially since the posture of the learner in looking up at a screen is quite different from that adopted when reading a book or making notes on paper. This kind of chair offers good lumbar support, and the swivel type improves circulation. As the office chair is vertically adjustable, it should be able to be adapted to most working surfaces without difficulty.

Also, there should be plenty of space for the learner to spread open an A4-size notepad to take notes. These are obvious minimum requirements which all too often are not met, and I stress that in my view these are far from being minor irritants which are not worthy of consideration — they can have a major negative impact on the learner, particularly the individual who is frightened of computers, confused by them, or who simply dislikes the notion of things mechanical.

4.8.2 Robustness
In the early days of CALL, it was not infrequent for a program to 'crash' if it was given unexpected input. A learner who opted, for example, for a menu item by typing out 'two' instead of '2', could readily cause a fatal software error in a program designed to cope only with integer input at that point.

Elementary error-trapping soon became the norm, but robustness should mean more than interrupting any errors that occur at run time. If the options on a menu are, say 1–4, the program should not accept keyboard input other than the digits 1 to 4. If you are asked to key 'Return' in order to move forward, no other key should be accepted.

On a higher level, field testing is essential to ensure that the CALL package performs in the manner which it is designed to do, and that unexpected errors do not occur. The designer of a package is the worst person to do the field testing, since it is not infrequently the case that he will subconsciously avoid taking an action which might cause a failure in the running of the package.

On the other hand, as I have already stressed, the linguist is the best person to write the package, given an appropriate skill level in program-ming. Robustness can be imperilled by communication problems between a programmer and a linguist whose skills are mutually exclusive.

4.8.3 Consistency

Both to minimize the possibility of inadvertent miskeying on the part of the learner, and in order to enhance a sense of structure in the interaction with the computer, it is essential to be consistent in the design of CALL software on a number of different levels.

The same set of keys must always be used for the same set of actions within the program, since failure to do so not only confuses the learner and causes his attention to be directed away from the learning process, it can also lead to inadvertent errors being generated, even to the point of files being deleted by mistake.

Consistency of the interface is also important on the level of maintaining a stability of relationship between the learner and the program with which he is interacting.

4.8.4 Non-threatening interface

Even in this age of information technology (IT), there are learners of all generations who are not comfortable in the presence of computing tech-nology, and for this reason alone it is essential that the physical and learning environment should be as non-threatening as possible.

Computer terminology should be eschewed wherever possible, and the program's model of the learner should recognize that non-computerate users are not conversant with simple necessary actions such as closing a file when it has been written to and the interaction is terminated.

At all costs, the word 'error' should never appear on the screen. No learner should ever be placed in a position in which he is made to feel both inadequate and with no strategy for extricating himself from a situation.

4.8.5 Modality of interaction

As we saw earlier, the way in which people and computers interact is very different indeed from that in which people interact with other people.

This concern for the most apposite modality of interaction should also manifest itself in what might be termed maximizing the noise-to-signal ratio to the benefit of the learner. On the simplest level, the novice might be informed, if he is to hit function key 9, where function key 9 might be located on the keyboard, in order to avoid the continuity of concentration in the learning process being intermittently interrupted by having to switch from a CALL learning task to a keyboard-scanning activity, which may well cause a fatal interruption in the learning process, and a sense of frustration with the computer and a losing of confidence in its potentiality as a teaching tool.

4.8.6 Flexibility

This demand seems the most reasonable of all, yet it is the most difficult to achieve — even in the context of operating systems HCI, it has proved to be an elusive objective. What I mean by flexibility is the requirement that the nature of the interaction should be such that the user should not at any stage feel either that he is being asked to go through a number of tedious stages with which he is either thoroughly conversant or which involve unnecessary repetition in order to arrive at an objective, nor on the other side of the coin faced with a situation in which the information state of the screen is impenetrable to him and he has no idea of where to go next.

This is not necessarily related to the novice or expert nature of the user, as one example will demonstrate. I have seen more than one example of CALL software in which questions like the following are put to the learner before the exercise can be started:

> What is your name?
> Do you want sound on/off?
> Do you want colour/black and white?
> Are you in question and answer/examination mode?
> Which type of question do you want to do?
> Type in the name of the file you want and press Return.

That is such a rich example of how not to interact with a learner that I shall have to restrict myself to a limited selection of remedial proposals. First, it may be acceptable to present those requests for information sequentially at the beginning of the first exercise in a session, but to have to repeat each tiresome bureaucratic detail at the beginning of every subsequent exercise is to regard the learner in an inflexible and mechanistic manner which engenders annoyance and is pedagogically counter-productive.

The obvious remedy to such a deficient interaction is to put up on screen the options after the request for the user's name with an indication that these are the defaults and that the user should simply press Return to accept them, or key in the appropriate number to make alterations. One simple further step that can be taken is to record the relevant information in a small file and load the settings last employed by a particular user.

The central challenge of flexibility, then, is to create what I should call a 'sliding scale' of options to match as closely as possible the anticipated level of familiarity with the system which the learner might possess (or, indeed develop) during a given session.

The first CALL package which I devised, targeted on a mainframe system, contained a module which enabled the teacher to key in and test new question and answer material within a matter of minutes. The principal problem which arose when I released this package for use by others was that their level of knowledge of the computer and what it could achieve varied enormously. The solution I devised was to provide the package with a user-switchable set of three verbosity levels:

> The highest takes the beginner through the procedures for inputting and editing data, and the teacher can then progress to a more terse level when familiar with the macro. (Last, 1979, p. 166.)

The system, although primitive, functioned moderately well at all three levels. But it was none the less clear even then that there is an inherent paradox in the functionality of any multilevel interactive interface, and it is one which it is far from trivial to resolve.

In fact, the preferred solution seems to be for most users to switch from one system to an entirely different system. A common experience in this respect has been the first Amstrad series of PC-compatible microcomputers, which offer both MS-DOS and the GEM environment (as well as DOS Plus). Typically, users would begin with the user-friendly pull-down menus in GEM, until they became conversant with the system, and at this point they would tire of the slowness and bureaucratic nature of the interface and switch to the more rigorous environment of MS-DOS, which although hardly user-friendly, is far more swift in operation and much more under the direct control of the user.

4.8.7 Length of interaction

There is clearly a point during a pedagogical interaction, whatever the medium being employed, at which the concentration of the learner begins to flag. There are a number of factors involved in this phenomenon. We as teachers are familiar with the fact that, by trial and error, it has become evident that an hour-long lecture delivered at a uniform pace without variation begins to lose its effectiveness by the halfway mark, and that the more proficient lecturer will deliberately inject a change of tone, a pause for breath or questions, at that juncture, or by some other means seek to vary the nature of the interaction.

A lecture tends to be a one-way process, unless questions are invited from the floor or posed by the lecturer, and this means that the productive skills of the learner are not demanded in any concentrated form. An interaction with a computer, by contrast, is a highly intensive and demanding experience, and one in which the effectiveness of the educational benefit begins to tail off after a relatively short time.

Early researchers into CALL, not surprisingly, did not initially recognize that the problem existed, since the kind of interaction involved was so novel, and because most of the early programs were question and answer tutorial type, the problem emerged in a heightened form. I quote from my own experience with mainframe CALL:

> The blunder I had made . . . was concerned with the excessive length of the test I had devised: it contained no less than forty-eight questions to be responded to. In my innocence, that seemed to me a quite reasonable total, but after several students had been found hollow-eyed and suffering from exhaustion at the computer terminals, it rapidly became clear that CALL is a highly intensive activity, and one in which the intense degree of concentration required can be held for only a relatively brief span before tiredness sets in and the process becomes counter-effective — not least because the learner has no idea of when, if ever, he is going to finish climbing the mountain ahead. (Last, 1984, p. 44.)

The learner gains an instant response from the computer to each input and, at the press of a button, the next question pops up on the screen. Hence a sense of urgency, of increasing pace can be unwittingly injected into the interaction, but even if this does not occur, the fact that the learner is having to participate positively throughout the session does mean that severe time constraints may be placed on the interaction.

The first, and most important, lesson which I learned from observing students working on the primitive drills which I had devised was that the interaction had to be broken down into short sub-units of around ten questions, in order to give the student a known subgoal to aim for which was close enough to stimulate effort rather than deter it. In addition, it is an impossible task to design every exercise in such a way that it is at the right level for every learner in the group at that particular stage, so that if a learner found the exercise too easy, he could be guided to more demanding work. If, on the other hand, the exercise proved too difficult, it was at least short enough to minimize any demoralization that might be felt, and encouragement could be given to try a remedial back-up exercise.

In addition, I also built in a panic button to allow the learner to abandon an exercise at any time, which once more removed unwarranted pressure. The learner felt that the learning process was under his control and not that of the computer, both from the point of view of pace and of level of difficulty, and this was of great importance in maximizing the efficiency of the interaction.

Breaking the tasks up into readily achievable subgoals actually had the additional beneficial impact of extending the overall length of useful interaction time to a full hour, although some learners would continue well beyond that time.

A further important HCI factor in extending the time of the interaction is that of varying the activity undertaken by the learner. It was possible in my system for the learner, for example, to preview any test, by listing all the questions and answers, and this less-demanding activity both enabled the learner to take a hard copy of the exercise for home revision purposes and to lower the intensity of the interaction for a short while. There is the inevitable disadvantage built into such a system that the lazy learner will find the least stressful path through the interactive process, but that is hardly either a new phenomenon or one inevitably bonded to CALL. The remedies, too, are too well known for me to rehearse them here.

There is one other aspect of the time of interaction which deserves a mention here. I found and continue to find that allocating a number of private study terminals which can be accessed at any reasonable time by the learner is of very positive benefit in that the learner can undertake exercises away from the constraints of a timetabled hour, and feels none of the pressure that a fixed interaction time can impose.

4.9   CONCLUSION

This chapter has sought to highlight a central but neglected aspect of CALL, and one which needs to be thoroughly understood since it represents the environment within which CALL interaction is to take place, and if the HCI is recognized as playing a key supportive role in the overall interaction, the scene can be set for CALL to function more effectively and with greater benefit to the learner.

Now we turn to the question of how to go about programming in CALL to a level beyond that of the first-generation packages, and to a consideration of the kinds of problems that arise in the selection of an appropriate programming medium, the quite different programming techniques that will be required, and then to an evaluation of non-algorithmic programming as it can be applied in the context of CALL.

5

The starting point

5.1 INTRODUCTION

It may well seem to have taken an inordinately long time for us to arrive at a chapter entitled 'The starting point'. However, it has been necessary to set the scene and detail the theoretical background to CALL, as well as to present an account of the current state of AI, and the much-neglected topic of the HCI, before arriving at a situation in which we can turn to consider the nature of AI CALL programming, and what marks it off from non-AI, or conventional programming.

There is a world of difference between a conventional computer program and one which has a measure of genuine AI about it. I use the word 'genuine' deliberately, because it might be claimed by some that a program like ELIZA has intelligent features to it, and I shall be examining those claims in a little while.

Let me take by way of example of a conventional program the French Pronouns Program I wrote for the BBC B microcomputer. I choose this example simply because it is obviously a program I know rather well. The manner in which such a program, or strictly speaking package since it consists of a suite of programs operated via a unifying menu structure, is designed and developed follows a pattern which is now pretty well established in the programming world.

The first prerequisite in conventional programming is to determine in detail what your objectives are before the computer is even approached. Naturally, those objectives have to display certain characteristics which will enable them to be processed by a computer program. These characteristics are that the entire programming process can be broken down into a number of logical, programmable steps, which in turn can be built up into a total system which is entirely deterministic. In other words, it is a step-by-step process of analysis followed by a mirror-image synthesis.

5.2 THE NEED FOR DECOMPOSABILITY

The decomposability of the problem into algorithmic subunits is essential, since the program which will be carrying out the procedures which have been constructed is only capable of coping with situations in which the choices are clear-cut, given a particular state of the program, and resolvable into a single course of action. This means that such procedures must be deterministic. In other words, for every initial state of the program the outcome must be identical. Put another way, two plus two must always equal four, and there should be no rough edges, no 'perhaps' or 'maybe' about the way in which the program progresses from initial state to conclusion.

This does not mean that the processes which are thus decomposed cannot be highly complex, nor that the initial — or, indeed, any intermediary — state cannot be varied, say, by a process of randomization. Using a random number generator is simply an extension of the range of possibilities that the program presents, not a kind of foreshadowing of 'intelligent' programming, although it may well give the learner that impression, and such a situation can be potentially very harmful to the interactive process, as our discussion of ELIZA will show. In addition, particularly when you apply randomization in building up sentence parts, for example, problems of grammatically accurate structures which are semantically absurd arise. What must remain unaltered in the program is the effect of each individual procedure itself: given a specified set of parameters when the program enters a procedure, it must always exit from that procedure in the same way every time.

This means that if the sentence which begins a demonstration or test in the French Pronouns Program is 'Le jeune homme donne du pain aux garçons', the object pronouns are always 'en' and 'leur', and they always have to be switched round to 'Le jeune homme leur en donne'. Given that input, no other solution is permissible or programmable, unless it be a pre-programmed variant word or phrase.

This is a key feature of non-AI programming and, as we shall see, the shift into the direction of AI programs implies a change at the centre, which can and does cause very substantial difficulties which research is far from beginning to resolve.

In randomizing those sentence patterns, I had to take care to avoid matching up incompatible subjects, verbs, objects and indirect objects. You may have felt that even the sentence quoted feels a little odd when non-contextualized, but to allow in the same cluster of sentence parts as a subject, say, the word 'le chien' would cause the good student to turn to laughter and the bad student to confusion. In both cases, confidence in the computer as a teaching medium would be substantially reduced. And such a data design error reminds us that there is always a danger in non-contextualized drills that structure, function and correctness are given their due, but that meaning comes a poor fourth. Meaning must always be accorded an appropriate measure of significance, since language is not the manipulation of formal symbols but a device for communication and interaction.

So, to expand on the requirement I gave at the beginning of this account that the project has to be planned out in detail in advance, that requirement applies, not just to the program, the steps of which are followed from beginning to end, but also to the data which is operated on by the program. It is just as essential to ensure that there are no potential absurdities or contradictions lurking in the data as it is to iron out all possibilities of a logical breakdown in the procedures of the program.

5.3 UNAMBIGUOUS, RULE-DRIVEN DATA

The other side of the deterministic coin, then, is that the data on which you are operating should not break the rules either. There should be no hidden actual ambiguities in the data which the program would be forced to resolve, not by some magical technique, but by dealing with the situation in the sequence which it is programmed to manage it, with unintended results.

Let me offer an example which does not lay claim to being absolutely watertight, in that you may argue that there are deterministic ways round this particular problem, but it does demonstrate what could happen when deterministic rules are applied rigidly in a non-deterministic situation. Take the following pair of sentences:

> The man rang up his brother from a phone box because he was going to be late home.
> The man rang up his brother from a phone box because he was waiting for him at home.

The question, obviously, in a program — or in any automated procedure — which sought to parse these two sentences, is how the personal pronoun 'he' is to be coped with. Say that the algorithm for this module runs like this: if you find a personal pronoun at the beginning of a subordinate clause of this kind, then search back in the main clause for an appropriate noun cluster. 'The man' is an obvious candidate, so the program would substitute 'the man' for 'he' in both cases. Now we 'know' that only in one case does it make sense for such a substitution to take place, and this means that we have been placed in a situation which cannot be resolved by context-free rules in an algorithmic manner.

The most that any algorithm could be expected to achieve in this situation is to report back that there are two clear candidates in each case for the resolution of the 'he' problem, but that it is not possible to determine from the surface structure, or indeed from any in-depth analysis of the sentence, which of the candidates is the winner in each case, or indeed if either is right.

There is a hidden trap lurking in the last paragraph. And that is, that the program must be sufficiently robust to know when it does not know the answer. Again to the linguist, this may seem so self-evident as hardly to require a mention, but in the context of the conventional computer program it can present some quite difficult challenges. If I may take by way of example another of my CALL attempts (again simply because these are the programs I know best), I devised a German Strong Verbs Program which had as its data all the German strong and mixed verbs, their principal parts, and English equivalents.

The package performs a number of different functions: it can be used as a dictionary look-up, either in English or German, or it can be used for testing the learner on verbs grouped by difficulty and in one or more of a number of tenses, from the simple present to the pluperfect subjunctive, with a variety of context-sensitive help procedures.

In writing the package, it became clear that there is relatively little difficulty in working outwards from fixed rules and within a clearly defined set of parameters. The program was given rules to work out the full forms of the tenses of each verb, and exceptions could readily be catered for by spelling out the form in full. Here, for example, are two verbs as stored in the database: one regular, one which displays consonantal as well as vowel changes:

    brech,i,a,,o,h,break
    geh,,ging,,gegangen,s,go

The infinitive is assumed in both cases to be regular, in that the 'en' ending is required. In the case of 'brechen' the vowel is modified in the second and third person singular present, in the case of 'gehen' it is not. In the imperfect indicative and subjunctive, 'brechen' simply changes the vowel to 'brach' and modifies it in the normal way in the subjunctive. On the other hand, 'gehen' undergoes a consonantal change. And so the rule-building process goes on, and with those unambiguously stated parameters each form of the verb can be generated. With a similar rule-based process, alternative forms like 'ladet' and 'lädt' can readily be catered for.

This means that as long as any kind of request is made of the program to create a form based on a known and unvarying set of rules, no problem will arise, even to being able to distinguish in the above two examples between the fact that one verb requires 'haben' and the other 'sein' (denoted by the initial letters) in the compound tenses.

The real moment of truth, as it were, comes when you try and reverse the process, and it is useful to pause here and consider in outline the kind of challenges we shall be facing in a later chapter. It presents no problem at all to the program even if you ask for the German for 'to go', when you are after one of a possible list of verbs ('laufen', 'gehen', 'fahren', and so on), so long as you have a strategy built into the program and/or the interface to cope with the situation. Working outwards from given rules can be extended to almost any point of complexity.

5.4   WORKING FROM EXAMPLES BACK TO RULES

What cannot be done at all so easily is to give an instance of a rule in operation, let us say 'er ginge', the imperfect subjunctive of 'gehen', and work backwards to the infinitive whence it came. Driving up a tree structure which was designed to work in the opposite direction can be quite a challenge, to put it mildly. Take that a step further, and allow the inputting of compound verbs, and the challenge becomes even greater. Here are two examples:

> umgeben
> gegenüberliegen

Generating the rules in the abstract and then feeding into them concrete examples of the rules in operation creates problems which, once again, the linguist dealing in terms of human understanding and human reactions, even by a relatively inexpert learner, finds it hard to recognize as such.

We instantly divide those verbs up into 'um-geben' and 'gegenüber-liegen', and thus determine that both are based on strong verbs which require 'sein' in the compound tenses. Equally, we recognize that, while the second verb is separable, the first can be either separable or inseparable, depending on context.

Teasing that conclusion out of a program which is designed on the lines of the German Strong Verbs program is, however, not such a trivial matter, and in fact I gave up my attempt to allow compound verbs to be analysed for one simple reason. Even given the fact that the most sensible approach is to try and break down these forms 'backwards', as it were, thus arriving at the same division as the human linguist into prefix and basic verb form, the other problems will not simply melt away. (If you work from the front of the verb, you may well determine that both have inseparable prefixes, 'um' and 'ge', and that the second verb is 'überliegen', a form not in the list and therefore assumed to be a weak verb.)

There is no way in which the program can determine whether the verbs are separable or inseparable, since both 'um' and 'über' can exist in either form. So, if we are to work from examples up to rules, a quite different strategy will have to be in place. We shall consider the possibilities and the dangers in a later chapter.

The outcome, then, of a situation which we have not designed the program to cope with, is either that the program delivers a 'result', which will be right or wrong depending on factors which have nothing to do with the merits of the programming procedures, or it will be forced to give up because it has been placed in a situation in which a conflict cannot be resolved within the design constraints of the program.

You will have noticed another feature of this kind of problem, and one which causes many humanists, and linguists in particular, to wonder what all the fuss over AI is really about. Surely, it might be argued, there is no problem over the two sentences, since we all 'know' that one 'he' refers to the man, the other to his brother. This, however, is precisely the point at which human thinking and computer programs diverge. What is so straightforward to us can become hugely complex and ultimately unresolvable if we seek to break the problem down into a number of discrete steps, as I have demonstrated with the two verbs in the preceding paragraphs.

Even if the situation can be resolved for this specific instance of ambiguity of reference back, there is no guarantee at all that any algorithm that has been so far designed will be able to cope with a related, but slightly different manifestation of the same problem. So this pair of sentences demonstrates the kind of difficulties confronting any attempt to move in the direction of AI programming.

It almost seems that we have to resort to the counsel of despair of having a one-to-one identity between rule and example, in other words, having a different rule for each and every manifestation of all the possible combinations to be covered by the program. And there are even cases where even that will not work, if you just consider two simple ambiguities in French and German, where the form 'je suis' has two quite different connotations (be and follow), and the form 'gestanden' could be the past participle of either 'stehen' or 'gestehen'.

This was precisely the area of greatest difficulty for the earlier MT workers. It is not too much of a challenge to arrive at a situation in which you have teased out the role and meaning(s) of the sentence elements, but if you are confronted with a difficult challenge in lexical disambiguation such as this, the way forward is not exactly straightforward.

5.5   KINDS OF KNOWING

There is another point, too, which we shall be examining in Chapter 6.8, and that is that it is all very well to say that we 'know' which 'he' is what. The mechanisms which enable us to know are far from being clear to us, and there is the additional complication of the kind of knowledge involved in such thought processes. What I mean by this is that 'knowing' is not simply a designation of a skill level that enables us to decompose the problem simply by throwing rules at it until it gives up before superior intellectual firepower. Knowledge signifies here understanding and mastering a hugely complex body of constantly shifting information, ideas, insights, and so forth, way beyond the immediate context of the problem. That includes, to go back to our original pair of sentences, 'knowing' that people almost never ring up their brothers from call boxes inside their own homes, and that 'je suis un éléphant' implies, 99 times out of 100, that one is following an elephant rather than one is an elephant.

Equally, that kind of knowledge is not cut and dried, unambiguously clear: the man 'almost never' rings, although if his home is a hotel with a call box in the lobby he might. The speaking elephant is a similarly unusual phenomenon, unless we are dealing with, say a cartoon film or some such similar situation.

To continue following the developmental path of the conventional, deterministic program: having broken the problem down into discrete steps, and having also determined what the limits of the program are — in the case of the French Pronouns Program, whether it would cope with negatives plus pronouns in compound tenses, or the imperative, positive or negative — the conventional process of run, debug and edit would then be repeated until the program had been as fully 'debugged' as possible, then subjected to beta-testing and finally released.

It is not necessary to go into details here about the structuring of the program, the way in which the procedures are modularized, nor to what extent and at which stages a top-down or a bottom-up approach is appropriate. These are matters of tactics rather than strategy: the important fact to recognize is that the problem comes first, the programming next. Then comes the process of testing until the programmer is satisfied that the program is 'finished'.

It is very tempting at this point to argue that I am inventing problems where none exist, since programs have surely already been written which have overcome far more complex issues than these, despite the reservations thrown up by the pair of ambiguous sentences I cited a little while ago.

The phenomenon is one which I would describe as the appearance of intelligence, as when someone exclaims 'Isn't it clever?' when a bank cash dispenser presents you with crisp ten-pound notes and a statement of your current balance, or an on-board car computer informs you that at the present rate of driving, you have fuel enough for the next five miles only.

5.6   THE CASE OF ELIZA

The program which is almost inevitably referred to in this context is ELIZA, and it is important to consider why such a program has had such an impact, why it caused such controversy when it first appeared, and why that reaction in turn caused its originator to stop short in his views of AI and reconsider them completely.

ELIZA was the brain child of one of the pioneers of AI, Joseph Weizenbaum, who began as a great enthusiast and believer in the achievability of the goals of AI, but has now become one of the strongest voices of caution about the way in which computers should or should not be employed in AI. And ELIZA played a key role in the reversal of his views.

At the time at which he wrote his controversial program in the late 1960s, Weizenbaum was interested in the question of communication between man and machine. The focus of his interest was to determine the appropriate modality of interaction which would enable a human and a computer together to solve a problem or perform a task. So Weizenbaum devised ELIZA. The name was taken, not surprisingly, from Eliza Dolittle in Shaw's play *Pygmalion*, for the illuminating reason that, while Eliza gave every appearance of having successfully been translated from the gutter into high society, there was no evidence of intellectual betterment on her part. She was simply acting out a role according to predetermined rules.

As for the program itself, let Weizenbaum in retrospect describe what it sought to achieve:

> ELIZA was a program consisting mainly of general methods for analyzing sentences and sentence fragments, locating so-called key words in texts, assembling sentences from fragments, and so on. It had, in other words, no built-in contextual framework or universe of discourse. This was supplied to it by a 'script'. In a sense ELIZA

was an actress who commanded a set of techniques but who had nothing of her own to say. The script, in turn, was a set of rules which permitted the actor to improvise on whatever resources it provided. (Weizenbaum, 1985, p. 188.)

So the essence of ELIZA was to feed the program data which would enable it to react in certain pre-programmed ways to text keyed in by the user. Unfortunately, the first script that Weizenbaum devised, parodied (that is the term he uses) the responses of a Rogerian psychotherapist to a patient undergoing the preliminary interviewing process. The choice was doubly unfortunate: first, because it involved mimicking an actual psychiatric technique, and secondly, because that technique lends itself so well to this particular program, because of the way in which the doctor responds to the patient's words and leads him along a line which should, in theory, home in on his deepest concerns and preoccupations.

This meant that ELIZA created a very passable illusion of responding 'intelligently' to the user. Let me quote part of a sample session which Partridge cites. ELIZA's responses are in capitals:

> I need some help, that much seems certain.
> WHAT WOULD IT MEAN TO YOU IF YOU GOT SOME HELP
> Perhaps I could learn to get along with my mother.
> TELL ME MORE ABOUT YOUR FAMILY
> My mother takes care of me.
> WHO ELSE IN YOUR FAMILY TAKES CARE OF YOU
> My father.
> YOUR FATHER
> (Partridge, 1986, p. 57.)

All very impressive-looking stuff, until you begin to analyse the reactions of ELIZA to the human input.

Without wishing to enter into an exhaustive analysis of the way in which ELIZA functions, the partial exchange above demonstrates three of the features of the program. First, it has built-in questions which can be posed in response to the existence of certain words, like 'help'. Other appropriate triggers would elicit a similarly formulated question from the computer.

Second, the program searches for particular keywords which it responds to as in the sentence about the family. The word 'mother' (or its synonyms or similar references to the father) triggers an invitation to the user to say more about the family. And thirdly, the program is given a number of tactics to cope with a situation in which (as in the last part of the exchange) the user either does not provide sufficient information for the program to move the interaction forward, or a sentence is typed in which contains nothing to which ELIZA is programmed to respond, in which case one of a series of non-committal sentences is generated.

The reason why I have lingered over this particular issue is that it demonstrates some of the major pitfalls which present themselves to any attempt at an 'intelligent' interaction between CALL learner and the computer.

The biggest danger in the user–computer interaction is that the computer is perceived as being more 'intelligent' than it in fact is. When the program reacts to an incorrect input by responding that the user has typed in the dative plural instead of the accusative singular, it may appear to be invested with grammatical knowledge which it does not in fact possess. Such an input would be easy for the program to monitor in cases where there is no ambiguity ('den Herrn' and 'den Herren', for example), but where one form serves both cases ('den Menschen'), the illusion can break down.

In such general circumstances, as in the case of ELIZA, it is not a matter of a program evincing 'intelligence', but rather 'cleverness'. It has been well programmed to respond, but the limitations remain.

On the other side of the coin there is a psychological problem to be considered; namely, that no one likes to feel cheated. That, I suspect, lies behind much of the over-reaction to ELIZA. Despite its obvious limitations, it actually seemed for a while as if a new psychiatric tool had come into our hands, and people convinced of the genuineness of what was supposed to be a harmless illusion were more than a little reluctant to admit that what they had witnessed was only a 'clever' computer program in action.

It is quite easy to demonstrate the limitations of ELIZA. If the program concentrates on the family, on worries and concerns about relationships and the rest, try — if you have access to a version of the program — interacting with it on a subject like shipbuilding or aeronautics, and you will see what I mean.

It is in my view a dangerous circular argument to propose that, even if the dog sings badly, the fact that it sings at all implies that there is genuine intelligence present. I quote from a recent paper on developing an intelligent syntax checker for CALL:

> Some element of intelligence has been convincingly demonstrated, often even on the humble micro, and the severest critics have thus been forced to repeatedly reduce the area where 'a mere machine will never be as good as a human being'. (Gallerly and Butcher, 1989, p. 83.)

There is no doubt that, as the years go by, computer programs will be devised and hardware environments developed which will transform the capabilities of those systems, but, leaving aside the social and other dangers which lie in the future, and which I discuss at the end of this book, I cannot accept that a performance rating can be equated with intelligence, unless, that is, you take a very narrow and mechanistic view of human intelligent behaviour.

5.7   THE TURING MACHINE

Even more famous than the ELIZA program in this contentious area of machine intelligence is the so-called Turing machine, which was the brain child of Alan Turing, a pioneer of AI who produced his theory way back in 1936. This is not the place for a detailed discussion of Turing's machine (which was never built) nor his Turing Test. Full accounts will be found in Haugeland (1985) and Weizenbaum (1985).

The basis of the Turing Test was to substitute a computer for a human being in a specially devised 'imitation game', and for it to be determined whether a computer or a human was playing. The fact that it might not be possible to tell the difference does not, however, mean that the computer has attained a human level of intelligence, simply that it has been adequately programmed for the task in hand:

> A machine can play the imitation game, but it can't think. (Gunderson, 1985.)

Simply because a machine can perform in a certain way, it does not mean that it is our intellectual equal. Gunderson goes on to argue that we tend to attribute intelligence to a machine that is capable of working out the monthly salaries for all the employees of General Motors in a matter of minutes, but we do not tend to follow this same path in 'the case of a swallow that returns in the spring to its place of nesting' (Gunderson, 1985, p. 49).

There is a hidden implication here that we are inclined, for whatever reason (perhaps our western infatuation with the machine, as was discussed in an earlier chapter), to invest a machine which evinces the least manifestation of independent thought, or its semblance, with the mantle of intelligence, and that in itself is a dangerous proclivity.

Because computers can add up faster than we can, and sort the words of the Bible into alphabetical order while we make a cup of coffee, that does not necessarily signify that they are in any way, either actually or potentially, our intellectual superiors.

5.8   CONCLUSION

So, non-AI programs, even though they may appear to display some of the characteristics of 'intelligence', are essentially deterministic, algorithm-based, and deal with a closed problem domain which is completely lacking in ambiguities and deals in black and white issues with no shades of grey between.

And, as we have seen, CALL has exploited these features in a wide range of programs which have carefully selected aspects of language that can be processed in these terms. From that point of departure, then, the question is how to move forward, and what kind of challenges face us in so doing. Fortunately, intensive AI research over the past decades has covered a lot of the ground for us, although much of the resultant outcome has been to demonstrate what cannot rather than what can be achieved.

The question is how to determine which techniques are available for us to move towards AI-type CALL. In many respects that is the wrong question to ask: the real issue is what are the problem areas which have been tackled and what are the difficulties which have appeared. In my view, the key aspects of AI as far as future CALL developments are concerned are four in number: problem-solving techniques, knowledge, modelling the mind, and the question of expertise.

To a considerable extent these issues overlap and contain with them other important aspects such as searching strategies and the kind of logic which AI programming demands, but I shall try and deal with them in as organized a fashion as possible. The first issue, then, is that of problem-solving techniques for AI.

6

Knowledge, heuristics, and modelling the mind

6.1 GENERAL SOLUTIONS TO SPECIFIC PROBLEMS?

In the context of problem-solving techniques, the first issue to be addressed is the fact that, in the course of the history of AI, there has been a distinct and seemingly irreversible shift away from the view that we possess general problem-solving strategies which we then apply to individual problem domains. The presence or absence of such strategies should, however, not be confused, particularly in language learning, with a general aptitude for languages. The efficiency of the mind in learning is quite a distinct issue from that of the way in which the mind functions.

In the past, a fair amount of stress in language teaching has been placed on aptitude and exploiting it, but it should not be thought that AI-like CALL can exploit aptitude in the same way, except in the broadest sense of seeking to encourage the learning process by every means possible.

But I return to the issue of problem-solving strategies, which are now regarded as domain-specific. In the 1950s and 1960s, however, the picture looked quite different:

> There is ... one common element in all of the work we have considered so far. This is a trend away from special purpose routines and toward more flexible and general purpose data structure interpreters. (Reitman, 1965, p. 124.)

At this stage in the evolution of AI research, it seemed the only reasonable approach to set about designing a General Problem Solver (GPS), which Newell and Simon developed from a program called the Logic Theorist (LT) in 1957. The ultimate objective was to formulate a theory of human behaviour.

The GPS works something like this. If you have a problem, this means that you have a goal or objective to achieve, and you are currently in some kind of initial state and about to proceed along the pathway from problem to solution. A set of operators exists which allows you to move from one sub-goal state to the next until finally you have solved your problem. The principal strategy would be to tease out the tangled threads of the various elements of a problem, and to isolate the general strategies which drive the problem-solving engine from the domain-specific 'objects' which constitute the problem and on which the 'operators' perform their problem-solving tasks:

> GPS ... was the first problem-solving program to separate in a clean way a task-independent part of the system containing general problem-solving mechanisms from a part of the system containing knowledge of the task environment. (Newell and Simon, 1972, p. 414.)

It all sounds so smooth and plausible, particularly the phrase 'in a clean way', which implies that all we have to do is to learn to see the wood for the trees and all our problem-solving difficulties are over. The reasoning techniques involved in this process are given the title of 'means–end analysis', which has a purposeful and scientific ring to it. But even a supporter of the GPS approach gives the game away when he admits that decontextualizing the cognitive elements of a structure almost inevitably engenders impoverishment of our understanding of how a system works:

> For it is the indirect connections among elements, connections which may be lost when an object is taken out of context,... which underlie the possibilities of compounding new direct connections between the given element and others in the network. (Reitman, 1965, p. 121.)

Despite built-in refinements, the GPS never attained a satisfactory level of performance:

> GPS was a dream come false. Its ideal of generality rested on several unfulfilled assumptions, of which two are most noteworthy. First, the basis plan presupposes that, under the skin, all problems (or at least all solutions) are pretty much alike. The second unfulfilled assumption ... is that *formulating* the problem is the smaller job, compared to solving it once formulated. (Haugeland, 1985, p. 183.)

However, it turned out to be the case that neither of those assumptions held water. In the first case, the techniques for moving from problem to solution have proven to be largely domain-specific, requiring knowledge and expertise about the problem domain in which the problem is to be solved, rather than wide-ranging techniques of general applicability. And in the second case, it is not setting out what the problem is in detail which poses the greater challenge; on the contrary, it is the solution techniques which constitute by far the more intractable area. The GPS assumes that all problems are technical ones which can be broken down by the application of the appropriate general techniques. For a detailed critique of the GPS, see Weizenbaum (1984, pp. 171ff), and Haugeland (1985, pp. 179ff).

There is another respect, too, in which the notions behind the GPS are doomed to failure, and that lies in the 'concrete–abstract distinction' (Partridge, 1986, p. 203). If a problem is chosen with care and acted out within the electronic confines of computer memory, then it is not impossible to resolve it in the abstract. But only a tiny class of problems is remotely like that.

The majority of problems, and this includes that of dealing with natural language, are far more complex and less well-structured. We are not dealing with controlled experimental circumstances, but with concrete situations in the real world which have to be solved in real time. Partridge contrasts a computer problem solving the famous monkey and bananas problem in the abstract (in which a monkey has to manipulate objects in order to grasp hold of a bunch of bananas which are initially out of reach) with a real, computer-driven robot seeking to deal with the arbitrary environment of reality, the errors that occur, the backtracking required:

> I don't think that the magnitude of the discontinuity between abstract and concrete AI can be overemphasized.... Any AI-system designer worth his salt will of course recognize that the concrete application will necessitate the addition of numerous checks and traps. But after-the-fact patching with such checks is not the same as preparing for them from the beginning, and designing the system to deal with the inherent uncertainties right from the start. (Partridge, 1986, pp. 204–205.)

This is precisely the kind of problem we face in CALL when moving from the comparative safety of drill and practice out to exploring, say, the application of CALL at the sentence level, where as the experience with the GPS shows, it is not simply a matter of making the algorithms more complex to cope with a situation which is different in degree. The situation is in fact different in kind and requires an entirely different approach if success is to be hoped for.

6.2   THE MICRO WORLDS

It is not, then, a simple 'technical' matter of scaling up, and this is precisely the area in which other early, and much-praised, AI experiments foundered. A concept such as that of the 'micro world' appears on the face of it very attractive. Take, for example, a simple declarative utterance in the target language which we may wish to process for a CALL program, resolve all the problems and issues which that sentence — and indeed that class of sentences — raises, and then 'all' you have to do is to scale the problem up by adding the complexities which allow you to move seamlessly from your 'micro world' to the real world.

Unfortunately, it does not turn out to be as simple a matter as that. Let us consider the most famous micro world of all, the unpronounceable SHRDLU simulated robot (the name derives from the title given to the computer program), designed by Winograd at MIT. Ironically, SHRDLU was primarily designed to experiment with communication between computer and human in natural English, but Winograd chose as his medium an imaginary world consisting of a number of blocks of different shapes and colours. It is the blocks world itself which has attracted the greater measure of attention. The program would be asked to put, say, the red block on top of the green block, and the program can also learn new vocabulary.

Like ELIZA, it appears at first quite impressive, but the real and fundamental deficiency is, as Haugeland and others have pointed out, the micro world itself. Ironically, what Winograd did was to seek to achieve a measure of AI by ensuring that everything in the micro world that could possibly have the rough edges and unpredictabilities of the real world are first removed. To borrow the phrase from Newell and Simon, the problem was 'cleaned up':

> SHRDLU performs so glibly only because his domain has been stripped of anything that could ever require genuine wit or under-standing. In other words, far from digging down to the essential questions of AI, a micro world simply eliminates them. (Hauge-land, 1985, p. 190.)

In addition, a micro world like SHRDLU has no real knowledge of its own environment. Weizenbaum underlines this fact by stating that:

> What Winograd has done ... is to build a machine that performs certain specific tasks, just as, say, seventeenth-century artisans built machines that kept time, fired iron balls over considerable dis-tances, and so forth. Those artisans would have been grievously mistaken had they let their successes lead them to the conclusion that they had begun to approach a general theoretical understand-ing of the universe, or even to the conclusion that, because their machines worked, they had validated the idea that the laws of the universe are formalizable in mathematical terms. (Weizenbaum, 1984, p. 196.)

So it is not true that, by stripping a problem of what appear to be the minor awkward side-issues and then breaking it down into its component steps, the problem can be scaled up to cope with the vagaries of the real world. As was the case with the first phase of MT, it was the minor side-issues which turned out to be the major, and in the last analysis unresolv-able, problems.

There is an important lesson here for linguists working on AI-like CALL, since we all typically start by protecting the learner from those awkward side-issues, but then we gradually introduce those complexities until the learner can cope with the problem in all its manifestations. The fact that we can achieve that with a human being does not mean that we can somehow transfer that process on to the computer without further ado. As we shall see when we come to deal with levels of expertise, there is no simple accumulative process which takes one up a single, unbroken path from beginner to expert level. And that parallels exactly the notion of the fallacy of the first successful step in AI, the notion that if you can solve the first bit of a problem (however small the bit may be), you are inevitably and unstop-pably on your way to solving the whole of the rest of it.

And, in the process of moving from the level of beginner through the various skill levels to the point at which a measure of expertise can be said to have been achieved, you will have noticed that one key element (perhaps the key element) has been absent from the discussion of techniques and strategies, and that is knowledge, which we shall be considering shortly.

6.3 ALGORITHMS AND HEURISTICS

So, having established that there are no general solutions to specific problems, I turn now to the techniques which are required to try and solve problems in an AI-like context. It is the non-specialist's broad assumption that all problems can be broken down into classical logical steps, decomposed into the algorithms I described in the previous chapter when discussing non-AI CALL programs. But even in the case of many programs dealing with a self-contained problem with inflexible rules, like chess, the algorithm is powerless to resolve the question as to what the computer's next move should be, simply on the basis that there is not sufficient time in the universe for each and every possible combination of moves to be followed through.

A selective, rough-and-ready technique has to be adopted, and this has been given the name of heuristics. It is really nothing grander than intelligent guesswork, and one good working definition comes from Newell, who states that heuristics:

> are rules of thumb and bits of knowledge, useful (but not guaranteed) for making various selections and evaluations. (Newell, 1983, p. 210.)

If a reasonably complex problem can be described, in part at least, in terms of searching a space for a solution, or at least a subgoal which moves one real step nearer a solution, then there are two broad searching techniques that can be adopted: depth-first, and breadth-first. The depth-first technique would be to apply a single criterion and pursue it as far as possible until either a solution was arrived at or, much more likely, we found ourselves in a dead end, and the breadth-first approach would, as its name suggests, involve tackling the problem across a broad front, one step at a time.

Take the analysis of the following sentence by way of example:

> In the fall we drove the flock up north.

If the strategy you adopt is to find a verb, then work round it to build up a sentence pattern which makes grammatical sense (we leave semantics to one side for a moment), the depth-first approach may come across 'fall', decide that it was a good candidate for the tensed verb, then examine 'in the', realize that there is no noun cluster after those two words, reject 'fall' as a verb and allow it as a noun, then take the 'drove' as the next candidate, and so on.

Breadth-first might consider all three possibilities of verbs in the sentence — fall, drove, flock — and move a step at a time, rejecting options as each fell grammatically by the wayside. It is quite evident that no algorithmic pattern exists which can cope with this kind of problem, not least because of the kind of logic which the algorithm presupposes.

Take, for example, a number of English nouns which an algorithm-based program has to mark as singular, plural and don't know, given a set of rules which states that 'nouns in English end in s'. Feed the program these words and see what it makes of them:

   mothers, fathers, children, cactus, fish, media, thinks

As you can see, the problem is far from trivial even given the regularity of English nouns (yes, I am aware that the last word in the list is not a noun — more of that in a moment). This means that the first attempt by the program to divide the words into what it has been told are singular and plural nouns might go like this:

   singular: children, fish, media
   plural: mothers, fathers, cactus, thinks

So, back to the drawing board to refine the algorithm to explain to the program that, after the initial sifting process into 's' ending and non-'s' ending words, each of the two lists has to be checked for anomalies. As you will recognize, these anomalies unfortunately for our algorithmic program fall into two categories: those which either state that the following nouns are exceptions, or that if a noun ends in 'us' it is singular — unless it is on a list of exceptions, and so forth.

But what the program cannot do is cope with two of the words on our list: fish and thinks. As we know, fish, like sheep, grouse, trout (and legal counsel) can be singular or plural, and the form of the word offers no clue as to which it is. The disambiguation process would only be possible if the word was contextualized and a heuristic technique of search was applied to determine whether or not the lexeme concerned is singular or plural.

Even more intractable is the word 'thinks', about which the algorithm-based program would almost inevitably come to the wrong conclusion, because it is not a noun at all. The situation would be even worse with a word like 'drinks', which could be either a noun or a verb form. What the program lacks to resolve that problem is knowledge, and it is to knowledge that we turn shortly.

First, though, to the main point about the algorithmic process we have been exploring: the reasoning involved has been preprogrammed into the computer, and is static and unchanging. The rules are couched simply in the form of a series of If...then...else patterns, a branching structure. If the noun has no 's' ending then it is not a plural unless one of a given number of predetermined exception conditions applies.

This non-AI reasoning is called monotonic reasoning, because in this kind of system the rules are unchanging, and reaching one conclusion never invalidates an earlier conclusion. Our earlier attempt with the sentence about moving the flock up north, however, involves a different, more difficult concept, that of non-monotonic reasoning in which the whole process is based on the possibility, indeed likelihood, that interim conclusions can be overturned.

The conclusion that 'fall' is a verb is invalidated because of a later conclusion that 'in the' requires a noun cluster and the only one within sight is 'fall', hence 'in the fall' is a prepositional phrase and 'fall', in direct contradiction to our earlier belief about it, is not a verb.

These, then, are some of the problem-solving tools we shall have to learn to apply with AI-like CALL: using rule-of-thumb (heuristics) instead of algorithms, we shall have to fathom out how to test out a belief, find it is fallacious, backtrack to the appropriate level (possibly not the beginning of the entire search process), and then set out on a different tack.

I should add that the problems do not by any means end there: if we return to the relative cosy comfort of the micro world of SHRDLU, you will find not only a monotonic belief system applied to it, but a simple logic in terms of positives and negatives cancelling each other out. The micro world is also a closed world. If, for example, you ask: 'Is the red box on top of the yellow box?' the answer is a simple yes or no. That is a neat and tidy explicit situation:

> The implicit representation of negative facts presumes total knowledge about the domain being represented.... Its opposite, the open world assumption, assumes only the information given in the data base and hence requires all facts, both positive and negative, to be explicitly represented. (Reiter, 1981, p. 124.)

The world of language is far from being neatly closed and self-contained, and the existence of these open worlds has forced many AI workers to abandon the techniques of classical logic which were adequate for the manipulation of concepts within a closed world.

6.4 NON-STANDARD LOGICS

Non-monotonic reasoning requires non-standard logics, not least because we are not dealing with a situation in which all the circumstances are explicit and clearly visible:

> Many-valued and fuzzy logics have been imported into AI to deal with areas of vagueness and incomplete information. Most expert systems, for example, are forced to take decisions when not all the facts pertaining to the decision are available. (Turner, 1984, p. 13.)

This introduces the notion of a situation in which we say, for example, not that 'fish' is singular or plural, but that in the given context there is currently a 75% chance that it is singular, and that that percentage will vary up or down as the program works its way through parsing and disambiguation phases to reach a firm conclusion about 'fish' and all the other issues to be resolved.

For a detailed discussion of classical versus intuitionistic approaches to non-monotonicity, see Turner (1984, pp. 59ff), who comes down against the 'classicists':

> We only need to reason non-monotonically where we are in a state of partial ignorance: some things are known but others are in doubt. If these observations are correct then any attempt to base non-monotonic inference on classical model theory seems intuitively unsound. (Turner, 1984, pp. 68–69.)

In his study of logics for artificial intelligence, Turner introduces a further element which adds another dimension of complexity to the non-monotonic reasoning process, and it is one which we are familiar with in language-learning situations. It is, if you like, the dynamic element injected by different times and circumstances. None of the patterns of language, apart, that is, from the cliché and similar manifestations, are set in concrete. Time and circumstances change what might be an appropriate juxtaposition in one context to what, in another, might be quite wrong. Such dynamic, or as Turner calls them, temporal considerations, 'have been given scant attention in the AI literature' (Turner, 1984, p. 78):

> In temporal logic, unlike classical logic, the same sentence may have a different truth-value at different times. (Turner, 1984, p. 79.)

There are two further complexities, in addition, which Turner does not explore, the first of which is that the unspoken assumption of much of the foregoing is that we are dealing with problems *seriatim*. In real life, however, that is rarely the case, and certainly not with understanding and producing language. There is a whole series of problems, some of which interact with other problems, others of which do not, which are constantly at different stages of resolution, and the assumed end state at which 'the problem' is satisfactorily resolved is the exception rather than the rule.

The second is the fact that, in human problem-solving, we are not only using fuzzy logics in real time, we are also exploring the problem at different moments at quite different levels, moving apparently arbitrarily from homing in on detail to taking a broad overview of the problem. In addition, we are not functioning with the 'intelligence' part of our minds switched on, and the other, 'emotional' part switched off. It is clear that, not just from a motivational standpoint, a holistic view of mind is the only one which can adequately explain, even if only in the most general terms, the way in which the mind functions.

Tikhomirov's study of the role of emotion in problem-solving indicates that 'an objectively right solution of a complicated mental problem cannot be obtained without emotional activation', and he goes on to argue that the moment at which the resolution of a problem appears in sight is one in which the emotions play a key role:

> The experiments showed that at a certain moment in the process of

the search for a solution every subject experiences a feeling of confidence that he has grasped the general idea of the principle of solution. (Tikhomirov, 1983, p. 161.)

And this key moment he calls the 'emotional solution' of the problem.

You will have noticed a common thread running through this discussion of AI-type reasoning, and that is that the move towards AI is a move away from determinism, which guarantees a correct result every time, towards uncertainty, towards a situation in which adequacy of performance is the criterion. Measuring computing on a sliding scale like this is an enormously difficult challenge, since we are now moving away from what computers and computer programs do well into an area which is alien to them, and one in which the human mind which they are seeking to emulate does not and cannot guarantee 100% accuracy of performance.

Being capable of functioning adequately despite errors in a dynamic, real-time world is something we as humans learn to cope with. Whether we can teach machines to do the same is quite a different matter, not least because, as we shall see in a moment, we lack any real measure of insight into the processes which allow us to perform as reasonably well as we do.

6.5   A TANGLE OF THOUGHT PROCESSES

Heuristics, problem-solving strategies and the question of knowledge, as we have seen, tend to become readily intermixed, but this is almost inevitable, the more we realize that the AI problem is not one of an interaction between discrete monolithic reasoning units, but a closely knit area in which the different elements are not only interacting in a dynamic way but also potentially changing roles. Take, for example, the question of knowledge in a problem-solving situation:

> I would say 'assimilation of the unknown into the known' is the basic heuristic of a cognitive system, as it is its central adaptive function. If we had unlimited computational power, we would not need to store as 'knowledge' the result of past successful computation for use in the future. (Cellérier, 1983, p. 142.)

That assimilative process implies that different kinds of knowledge will need to change roles at different stages of the problem-solving process. What starts off as declarative knowledge (a factual element) may well, in combination with other elements, become part of procedural knowledge (knowing about what to do with the facts), and develop onwards into meta-knowledge (knowledge about knowledge). Those in search of a simple procedure for AI will be disappointed indeed:

> Procedures and structures are two related components of all cognitive activities. Every structure is the result of a procedural self-

destruction, and every procedure makes use of some of the aspects
of structures. (Inhelder, 1983, p. 135.)

There is, then, little sign of the 'clean' solution favoured in the past.

6.6   MODELLING THE MIND

One of the greatest challenges of AI is that of modelling the human mind.
The mind can be considered as a 'black box' into which data is fed and out of
which actions and so forth emerge. One objective of AI is to form a bridge
between the input behaviour, if you like, of the brain, and the output
behaviour, to explain satisfactorily what goes on inside the box, or at least to
emulate it in a functionally satisfactory manner.

The first, and most obvious, point to make is that the human mind
functions in a world which is many, many times more complex than anything
a computer program currently devised could begin to cope with in a
sufficiently efficient manner for it to be able to survive.

The second point is that the human mind evidently does not operate on
the von Neumann principle of a single stream of instructions being executed
in sequence. Human vision, for instance, requires huge parallel-processing
powers, and this feature of the human mind can be generalized across all its
functioning range:

> What distinguishes human-like intelligence from machine-like
> intelligence is the human ability to use a very large amount of
> diverse material in very different ways at virtually the same time —
> that is, simultaneous processing. (Huntsman, 1981, p. 24.)

Coping with such vast amounts of information in real time brings with it a
number of implications about the nature of the human mind. First, the
concept of 'faculty psychology' has fallen out of favour; that is, the notion
that we have general faculties such as judgement, logic and so forth which
are applied to specific tasks. Given the experience with the GPS, this is
hardly surprising. Our faculties are, then, not horizontal, but vertical,
task-specific.

The second implication is that much of the processing that takes place
has to be entirely unconscious, and indeed beyond our conscious control.
Imagine being burdened with the awareness of the way in which low-level
processes work out the shapes of these letters and words as you are reading
them, and then sensing how each completed word recognized is sent off to
another part of the brain for semantic and lexical processing, and you will
readily recognize what I mean. In addition, we cannot control these
processes:

> The operation of the input system appears to be … inflexibly
> insensitive to the character of ones utilities. You can't hear speech
> as noise *even if you would prefer to*. (Fodor, 1983, p. 53.)

Given the fact, then, that 'much the greater part of human information processing is undoubtedly 'unconscious', (Allport, 1980, p. 48), it is not going to be a trivial matter to gain insights into how they function, let alone model them. Such processes are 'informationally encapsulated' (Fodor, 1983, p. 70), in other words we simply do not have conscious access to them, but only to the output which they generate.

On a purely empirical level and even without reference to AI, this is a powerful model of the processes of foreign language skills acquisition, in that the learning process is in large measure trying to isolate these low-level processes, teach them in a conscious fashion, and then allow them gradually to be absorbed as informationally encapsulated unconscious processes, so that we can exercise our productive faculties in a foreign language without being conscious of the processes involved, thereby allowing our conscious mind to be in strategic control of the speech processes rather than concentrating on whether the endings are right or the words in the correct order. And indeed this model of the functioning of mind maps very neatly on to the notion of advancement from novice to expert which we shall be examining shortly.

6.7 LOW-LEVEL ENCAPSULATED PROCESSES

If these informationally encapsulated processes are to be fast, they must also be fairly unsophisticated, otherwise they again would slow down brain functioning, particularly in time-critical areas such as vision and hearing. One common thread in studies of how these processes work is the concept categories, which are the highest levels of abstraction in a particular category. Fodor again, this time quoting the work of Rosch:

> Basic categories are typically the most abstract members of their implication hierarchies which subtend individuals of approximately similar appearance…. So, roughly, you can draw something that is just a dog, but you can't draw something that is just an animal; you can draw something that is just a chair, but you can't draw something that is just furniture. (Fodor, 1983, p. 96.)

So the basic categories of 'dog' and 'chair' are useful to these low-level processes because they represent the most abstract members of a particular class which they can meaningfully process. Once again, we appear to be on familiar ground: the concept of word fields, which has been around in language teaching for a very long time, once more maps neatly on to the perception of the psychologists.

This scenario of low-level processing beyond the reach of the conscious mind brings in its train a hugely complex network of problems, such as the control mechanisms for the system to function properly, the way in which some information is ignored, other information accepted, and yet further information sent back for reprocessing. This is particularly the case with the human mind which is constantly functioning in real time:

> If a system is spontaneous and dynamic, time pressure results,

influencing relative complexity and together with a multicompo-
nent goal situation, raising the necessity to form points of main
effort, that is, to concentrate on certain goals and aspects of the
system. (Dörner, 1983, p. 93.)

Then, recognizing just how little progress has been made in this direction, he adds a couple of pages later that a 'theory of asking the right
questions' would be of the greatest value.

Trying to model the mind to its full extent, then, is something of a
daunting task, and it has been argued, probably not within our grasp at all,
because of the very way in which the mind functions. This is not least the case
because there appears to be little knowledge of or agreement on what
happens to the information after it has been processed outside the control or
knowledge of the conscious mind. Allport tends to the view that there is no
overall controller in charge of the mind. His basic assumption is as follows:

Processing and memory-capacity is distributed throughout the
nervous system over millions of special-purpose 'cognitive
demons'. (Allport, 1980, p. 32.)

By demons he means autonomous pattern-detectors. Fodor, on the
other hand, comes up against the frontiers of knowledge, as it were, in trying
to balance the modularity of the low-level processes against the holistic
nature of the central conscious processes. And he concludes:

The limits of modularity are also likely to be the limits of what we
are going to be able to understand about the mind, given anything
like the theoretical apparatus currently available. (Fodor, 1983, p.
126.)

There are, however, more optimistic voices. Lavorel, for example, is
fascinated by the challenges and problems thrown up by the way in which
cooperative computation, as he calls it, on a dynamic basis (the mind learns
as it goes along) presents a possible model for advance:

The principal lesson which has been learned from all these studies of
man's remarkable ability for knowledge of the world and for
schemas of acts is that intelligent performance is not simple and
deterministic. It varies because it is economical, task determined,
and permanently controlled. (Lavorel, 1981, p. 233.)

So he sees the possibility of a way forward, once the notions of dynamic
growth and development of the system and distributed parallel processing
are recognized, and presumably, once we learn how to program them.

I have spent a little while examining these issues because it is important
to recognize the size of the challenge that confronts anyone who seeks to
import AI techniques into CALL in any but the most half-hearted manner.
There is no doubt that the time has not yet come — and may never arrive —
when we can model the functioning of the mind in such a way as to provide a

satisfactory and challenging pedagogical environment for the CALL learner.

What does emerge, though, are a number of clues as to how some progress in the direction of AI-like CALL can be made. The point of greatest interest for me is the notion that the novice learner is developing on a conscious level (and in an increasingly organized manner) what in the expert become the unconscious and informationally encapsulated processes which feed into the higher level workings of the conscious central processor (if there is one, that is).

Before we examine this further, however, we need to consider some of the problems thrown up by the 'dynamic' aspect of the human mind, the way in which knowledge is acquired and increased.

6.8 THE PROBLEM OF KNOWLEDGE

Knowledge, it has frequently been argued, is one of the central characteristics of 'intelligence', in so far as it is possible to determine it. Let us first explore some of the issues involved by means of an imaginary interaction between man and machine.

The questionings about the nature of intelligence as applied to the computer are convoluted in the extreme, and make difficult reading. However, a principal philosophical objection to the paradoxical phrase 'computer intelligence' can be summed up in the simplest of all interactions with a computer, one which everyone learns on taking the first tentative steps in BASIC. The exchange goes like this:

>Computer: What is your name?
>User: Fred
>Computer: Hello, Fred

The problem can be stated in these terms: the response 'Hello, Fred' by the computer is not an intelligent response, since the computer does not 'know' the name Fred, it only has stored in a string memory location a bit-pattern which when converted into characters on the screen comes out as 'F' plus 'r' plus 'e' plus 'd'. If Fred lied about his name and dubbed himself Freda, the exchange would not alter:

>Computer: What is your name?
>User: Freda
>Computer: Hello, Freda

The difference between computer and human being lies in the 'intelligence' which would allow the computer to say: 'Don't be ridiculous. You can't be called Freda. You have a moustache.'

And it is at this point that the reasoning becomes convoluted. Let us now place a TV camera on top of the computer monitor, face it at the moustached user, load a program with pattern-recognition capabilities, and *then* the exchange may take the form of a rejection of Freda on the grounds of a moustache. But the addition of a 'sense' of sight does not make for intelligence, unless intelligence can be isolated out from other essentially human characteristics and 'taught' to the computer.

Let us consider another possible exchange:

Computer: What is your name?
User: Anastasia
Computer: That's an odd name. I've not heard of it before.

The essential difference about this exchange and an unintelligent 'Hello, X' when X is typed into the computer is that the computer now appears to have one essential constituent of intelligence at its disposal; namely, knowledge. If the computer has no knowledge it cannot possibly react intelligently. A human being, however 'intelligent', who knows nothing about powered flight would be completely at a loss when asked to distinguish between QFE and QNH, or VFR and IFR. The same applies in the computer exchange; if the computer has no knowledge, however limited of:

(a) what a name is;
(b) common English names;
(c) 'world knowledge' in this field,

it would not have been possible to piece together the response we postulated: 'That's an odd name' implies, typically, that the word 'Anastasia' has been checked to determine whether it begins with a capital letter, then against a list of names known to the program, and the second part of the response indicates that the computer has not found the name in its list.

At this point, one of two things could happen: the program might continue with the next part of the interaction sequence, an 'unintelligent' response, or it could seek to add new knowledge to what it knows already.

By comparing 'Anastasia' with names already in its database, it would not be difficult in this case for the program to conclude that it is a girl's name, on the gounds that it ends in 'a' and that there is a fuzzy match between 'Ana-' and 'Anne' which is a common feature of related names. The exchange continues:

Computer: Is it a girl's name?
User: Yes

Now the name is added to the database, and the next exiled Russian princess to use the program would be greeted with a *different* interaction sequence:

Computer: What is your name?
User: Anastasia
Computer: That's an unusual name for a girl. I've only come across
it once before

So knowledge, an essential feature of intelligence, has two important characteristics: (a) it is modified and extended by experience, and (b) it is linked in a number of ways with previously acquired knowledge.

Both computer and human being could now answer the questions: give me a girl's name with four 'a's in it, or: give me a name with more than eight letters (although the answer in this case may not, of course, be Anastasia — that would depend on previously acquired knowledge and the way in which this knowledge is achieved).

6.9 KNOWLEDGE ACQUISITION

The problems of knowledge acquisition are, as we know from our own experience, far more complex than that. Take, for example, this interaction sequence:

> Computer: What is your name?
> User: Azzzza
> Computer: Hello, Azzzza. That's an odd name. I've not heard of it before. Is it a girl's name?
> User: Yes

Two issues arise here: the first is that we all 'know' that, unless we are dealing with some remote Martian tribe with obscure consonantal clusters, it is unlikely in the extreme that any word, let alone a name, could contain four 'z's one after the other. But it is at this point that the argument begins to become circular: if the program was provided with a knowledge of consonanted clusters, it would reject Azzzza. However, on those grounds, it would 'accept' Alermia as a girl's name, although that, as far as I know, is my invention.

The key lies in the 'as far as I know': in using computers for learning purposes with knowledge, it is prudent to ensure that the knowledge contained in the program is sufficient to cope with the user's input and that the appropriate strategies are applied where this is not so.

This leads to the second of the issues raised by the Azzzza name: the computer now has in its knowledge base an item of incorrect knowledge.

At this point, computers and human beings appear to part company. A human being finds its easy to cope with incorrect knowledge or even partly assimilated knowledge and to correct or adjust the database in the light of new knowledge. A computer program can find it very difficult to cope with incorrect knowledge, and even more difficult to recover from error without crashing altogether.

Human beings might almost be described as computer programs running in a failed state, and it is tempting to pose the question as to whether it is worth attempting at all to write intelligent programs on a computer, since it is so manifestly lacking in intelligence.

As I indicated earlier, these arguments readily become circular, not least when we are considering an issue like the nature of human thinking, about which we appear to have precious little knowledge at all. Self is quite correct in posing this question about a learning package which purports to evaluate political issues:

How could a computer program make sensible judgements about

political popularity when we know virtually nothing about it at all? (Self, 1985, p. 46.)

The trouble with most knowledge is that it is a far more messy business than that, and on a number of grounds.

6.10   DIFFERENT KINDS OF KNOWING

First, the quality of that knowledge is rarely absolutely guaranteed. Consider the following statements, all allegedly referring to the same characteristic, knowledge:

(1) I know that two and two make four.
(2) I know that Fred is calling round tomorrow.
(3) I know that my Redeemer liveth.

It is hardly necessary to labour the point that there are three radically different kinds of knowledge all masquerading as the same kind of characteristic. In fact, the second and third of the three 'knows' could, and perhaps should, be replaced by the word 'believe'.

So here, too, there is no 'clean' solution. And this is particularly true in the case of knowledge in problem domains where the knowledge required is highly context-sensitive, about as remote from the reach of the GPS as you could imagine, and that includes among its chief members the understanding of natural language:

> If one accepts this context-sensitivity viewpoint, then current practical AI software is just those AI problems (or components of AI problems) that are only loosely coupled to their contexts. The highly context-sensitive problems, like natural-language understanding, and components of AI problems, such as self-explaining in expert systems, are just the AI problems that are still firmly in the research domain — except for some very limited and rigidly constrained special cases. (Partridge, 1986, p. 23.)

Our exploration of problem-solving techniques, heuristics and knowledge, then, has not yielded a rich harvest of simple solutions to the problems of AI in CALL. In fact, there are clearly a number of 'no-go' areas which it would be foolish for us to seek to devise production versions of CALL, since robustness and integrity of the HCI are critical in any learning situation. But all may not be doom and gloom. There is one area which appears to be much more promising than those we have examined so far.

Of all the various fields of AI endeavour there has been one which seems to have been more successful than the rest, and that is the area of expert systems, but here too we come face to face with another problem of scaling-up: the lack of a smooth continuum between novice and expert.

7

The potential of expert systems

7.1 INTRODUCTION

I turn now to consider probably the most practical route forward for CALL into AI, that of the expert system.

The concept underlying the expert system is, on the face of it at least, not only very attractive but one which appears to be well within the bounds of achievability. The objective of an expert system is to transfer the skill, knowledge and experience of a human expert onto a computer system in such a way that the computer can emulate the behaviour of the human expert — and also explain how it comes to its conclusions.

It will have taken a human expert many years of study and hard work to arrive at an advanced level of competence in his or her field (consider the example of a medical consultant in a particular field of treatment), and all that skill and knowledge would instantly be lost if the expert fell under the proverbial bus. The whole expensive and time-consuming business of training a replacement would have to start all over again. A much more cost-effective solution would surely be to extract the expertise from the human expert and inject it into a computer. Then all you would have to do is to key in the appropriate information and the computer would come up with a more or less instant response.

In addition, of course, expert systems would be more consistent in their diagnoses than human beings, they would never come into work with a hangover, nor would they ever go on strike for higher pay. Replacing awkward human beings with docile robots is a theme to which I shall return at the end of this book. Here let us merely consider the possibility of taking human expertise and computerizing it.

7.2 WORKING EXAMPLES

First, let me consider the successful practical implementation of expert systems. Given the amount of publicity engendered, one might expect both that there would be a large number of such systems extant, and that they would be performing complex high-level tasks with consummate ease. But the reality is less than inspiring.

Three representative systems which have achieved a measure of success are MYCIN, PROSPECTOR, and R1. For an accessible and balanced account of expert systems, see Alty and Coombs (1984).

MYCIN and PROSPECTOR have quite a lot in common, despite the fact that they are dealing with quite different problem domains. The former is a system designed and evolved at Stanford University as a means of assisting physicians with the diagnosis and treatment of infectious diseases. PROSPECTOR, on the other hand, is a tool to assist geologists:

> It was designed to provide three major types of advice — the evaluation of sites for the existence of certain deposits, the evaluation of geological resources in a region, and the selection of the most favourable drilling sites. The program was developed by SRI International in association with geological consultants and the US Geological Survey. (Alty and Coombs, 1984, p. 103.)

What both systems have in common is the fact that neither is dealing with hard and fast facts, but with probabilities. Of course, each works with production rules which are basically of the type: IF something is true THEN do something else, where we are not dealing with absolute truths, but what are known as CFs, certainty factors. The Boolean expression is typically more complex than a simple IF true THEN.

PROSPECTOR has actually been tested against the performance of expert geologists, and it appears to have performed more than adequately:

> The evidence demonstrates clearly and extensively the usefulness of PROSPECTOR not only for evaluating regional mineral potential, but also for actually quantifying the credibility and stability of its conclusions. Given the variabilities and uncertainties inherent in the task of resource assessment, the PROSPECTOR methodology introduces a powerful new tool by which to obtain assessments significantly more objective, repeatable, uniform, self-calibrating, detailed, and open to public inspection (hence defendable), than those presently available using other methods. (Gaschnig, 1982, p. 319.)

Of course, the 'success' of PROSPECTOR is conditioned by the quality of the information which it is provided with about any given site. If, as it seems, that quality is high and the level of detail more than adequate, the success of the program is not surprising, since its judgement is based upon tried and tested techniques applied to good-grade information.

MYCIN equally uses what are, in its case, called 'certainty factors' similar to those employed by PROSPECTOR, which also applies Bayes's Theorem, a method of calculating probabilities on the basis of past events. In both cases, the functioning of the system is to a considerable extent domain-dependent, which given what we have discovered about the specificity of knowledge and the skills which manipulate it, is hardly surprising. But MYCIN has sufficient in common with related subject areas that an expert system shell has been constructed called EMYCIN (empty MYCIN) which has been applied to related problem domains.

In common with many expert systems, and particularly important in the context of medical diagnosis, it is possible to ask MYCIN how and why it has arrived at its conclusions, and since MYCIN is constructed on the basis of a combination of production rule and certainty factor — IF patient not breathing THEN there is a 100% certainty that he is dead — it is a relatively straightforward matter to persuade it to retrace the steps by which it arrived at its diagnosis. However, like all current expert systems, MYCIN does not actually 'know' anything:

> Whilst the questioning facility in MYCIN is quite powerful, it is limited to reasoning about the immediate vicinity of the MYCIN reasoning state during the consultation. Furthermore, there are many knowledge aspects which MYCIN knows nothing about, e.g. why is pseudomonas a bacterium? It has no explicit causal knowledge of the domain of interest. (Alty and Coombs, 1984, p. 101.)

So MYCIN has been tolerably successful as a research tool, PROSPECTOR not surprisingly more so, but most successful of all has been a system called R1, which owes its success again to the nature of the facts which it is manipulating.

What R1 does is to work out a viable VAX-11 computing system based on the requirements drawn up by the salesman and customer. The output is in the form of diagrams. The program decides if the configuration makes sense, and if it does, it tries to produce a working diagram for the components.

After difficult developmental problems, R1 achieved a success rate in 1981 of more than 90% in designing systems, and its work was extended to more complex systems. As Alty and Coombs point out, it was developed in the teeth of a great deal of cynicism and caution among traditional engineers and it is a credit to the researchers that it achieved what it did (Alty and Coombs, 1984, p. 161).

Purely on the basis of experience rather than on experimental results, it seems that if an expert system handling matters as solid as printed circuit boards (PCBs) and wires and all the other components of computing can face considerable difficulties, how much more intractable are the problems of designing an expert system that can cope with even a relatively modest subset of natural language. That is a topic which we shall be examining in the next chapter.

7.3   ANATOMY OF AN EXPERT SYSTEM

We turn now to consider how such programs function in order to determine how, if at all, they can be applied to CALL.

The problem of designing an expert system breaks down into a number of sub-tasks, the first of which is finding a way of converting human expertise into a series of modules of some kind which can be entered into a database for subsequent extraction. We have already considered the issue of expertise being domain-specific and have discussed the failure of concepts like the GPS to cope adequately with such situations. Given, then, that expertise is specific to a particular problem domain (that the concert violinist's skills cannot be adapted in such a way that he can be translated into an eminent brain surgeon, and vice versa), a number of difficult issues arise in extracting such expertise.

The first is the question of the nature of the knowledge which is being extracted. Knowledge about a particular field can be broken down into two categories: procedural and declarative. An example of declarative knowledge in a car mechanic, for example, is: I know what a carburettor or a sparking plug is. Procedural knowledge comes under the heading: I know how to remove them and trouble-shoot them. It is, of course, by no means a straightforward matter to devise a hard and fast line of demarcation between the two kinds of knowledge.

It could be argued that there is a third category, metaknowledge, that is, knowledge about knowledge, but that can be also regarded in terms of the program that is to drive the expert system when it is interrogated.

There is the additional practical problem of ensuring that the system performs within any time constraints that may be placed upon it, to which I have referred in an earlier chapter. In this context, I cited earlier the example of an on-board car computer that takes too long to recognize approaching traffic lights, and the medical diagnostic program that solves the problem, but not quickly enough to save the life of the patient.

The difficulties with these two types of knowledge emerge as soon as you attempt to draw neat distinctions between them. Knowing what and knowing how to often seem to be hopelessly entangled one with another, and when it comes to breaking procedural knowledge down to a series of steps in an algorithmic process, a further level of difficulty comes to light.

At first sight, however, there hardly seems to be any problem at all:

> Reasoning (on the computational model) is the manipulation of meaningful symbols according to rational rules (in an integrated system). (Haugeland, 1985, p. 39.)

But any area of what appears to be 'reasoning' which involves a high degree of human skill may well run into the kind of difficulties which were encountered by early researchers into MT. The model appears to break down at a certain level of complexity, although at first sight it seems that it should not do so. The line of argument goes like this: if knowledge can be decomposed into basic units of step-by-step or algorithmic stages, then an expert is surely doing no more than functioning in a similar way but at a much higher level:

> The belief is that the higher the level of structure that can be matched or recognized, the more conceptual ground can be covered in one inferential leap. (Hayes and Michie, 1983, p. 42.)

However, it is argued by many researchers, and I concur with this view, that the expert does not operate in a logical, algorithmically decomposable, step-by-step, rule-based mode at all. He does not mentally flowchart a problem and then systematically set about solving it. Nor does he even perform in the alternative, heuristic-based methodology. Knowledge engineers, as the people whose task it is to extract knowledge from the experts have been called, have found it extraordinarily hard to persuade experts to articulate how they function in their problem domain. Not only do experts appear to have a deplorable lack of self-insight into their own reasoning processes (from the knowledge engineer's point of view, that is), it appears to be the case that reason is not the normal modality of the expert at all.

Indeed, it has been argued on more than one occasion that to try to persuade an expert to break his mental and physical functionings down into a series of logical steps is tantamount to demanding that he should stop conducting himself as an expert at all, and start behaving as a novice, who first learns his trade by imitating or learning in such a manner. We are clearly back at the logical impasse of the algorithm which I discussed in Chapter 5. And, even more depressingly for the knowledge engineer, there is no simple upgrade path by which a novice can be taken from the first stages of insight into a given problem domain to a point at which he can be declared expert. As teachers we are all familiar with the phenomenon: we can teach a group of students with all the skill at our disposal as experts ourselves, but only those few gifted students will be able to rise to a level of competence at which they become experts themselves, and the process by which this transition takes place is far from evident. It is obviously some combination of in-built ability and study and application, but what that combination may be is both elusive in the extreme and in any event varies wildly from one individual to the next.

For me, the most serious logical flaw in the attempt to turn computers into 'experts' is the question of talent or giftedness. If it were possible to turn mere computers into experts via a programming exercise, then surely it would be possible to do the same to human beings, to program all of us to become space-shuttle pilots or concert pianists. In addition, we should not allow ourselves to be deluded by some of the proponents of expert systems into believing that what they have created are real expert systems at all. The programs are operating 'in theory', like SHRDLU, are being fed facts and figures, and are coming up with hypothetical solutions to the questions posed. There is no question of the computer actually taking the patient's pulse, looking into his eyes, evaluating his condition in the same kind of way that a real medical practitioner would. It is all done in the abstract, *in vitro*.

7.4 THE PARADOX OF EXPERTISE

So in a sense, trying to graft human expertise onto a computer is a contradiction in terms. The complexities of the issues involved are neatly encapsulated in an example given by Alty and Coombs. The example they quote is that of the dry-stone wall builder:

> The opening of the task is characterised by a large pile of different-

sized stones. The expert wall builder does not know at the outset how and when he will select stones for the wall. Periodically he reviews the current state of the wall, the stones left, and selects an appropriate short-term strategy which may involve backtracking (taking stones off again). With an identical set of stones he may never actually build the same wall twice. (Alty and Coombs, 1984, p. 36.)

The expert, then, almost seems to muddle along without any clear theoretical basis. His work is conditioned to a large extent by 'experience', by having built many such walls, day by day, for years on end. In addition, he is not working with clear-cut issues, but with the balance of probabilities. Maybe three or four stones look promising at one particular stage of the wall building, but it is not until a later stage that the original choice will turn out to have been wrong. Then the human expert knows how far he has to backtrack through his task in order to remedy the faulty piece of building, but by then the other stones which had proved promising may have been used in another part of the wall. The complexities appear to be unending, the potential of computerizing the task dwindling rapidly as we consider each twist and turn in the wall-builder's work.

And another important fact emerges from that example which under-lines the differences between human and computer, and that is that no two human experts would come to exactly the same conclusions, and in fact a great deal of human expertise is 'topped up', as it were, by group discussion or taking a second opinion. If the computer medical expert said you were going to die, there would be no point in asking for a second computerized opinion. This is no more than an extension of what happened on Black Monday in 1987 when all the expert computer systems were triggered by a fall in stock market values to sell and thereby made the situation far worse than it would ever have been in the bad old days of manual systems.

Expert behaviour is not predictable. It cannot be decomposed into a number of predetermined steps. Papert, in his loosely argued and unaccoun-tably influential book *Mindstorms* takes the opposite view, or at least I think he does. It is what he calls an epistemological approach to the concepts of knowledge, intelligence and expertise, but it is all tangled up with his infatuation with LOGO and conviction of the centrality of mathematics:

> Two fundamental ideas run through this book. The first is that it is possible to design computers so that learning to communicate with them can be a natural process, more like learning French by living in France than by trying to learn it through the unnatural process of American foreign-language instruction in classrooms. Second, learning to communicate with a computer may change the way other learning takes place. (Papert, 1980, p. 6.)

His view is reductionist in the sense that the movement towards expertise is both regarded as one from the general to the particular, and also can be encapsulated in the phrase that 'to learn is to acquire a program' (Dreyfus and Dreyfus, 1984, p.43).

Contrary to such a perception are the views of writers like Dreyfus and Cooley. It may be valuable to consider first the views of Cooley, who is concerned in his book *Architect or bee?* more with questions of employment from a socialist stance than directly with questions of AI and expert systems as such. But it is illuminating to note that there appears to be developing a considerable convergence of opinion among researchers in a whole range of different fields, from social theoreticians to scientists exploring the notion of 'chaos', that the reductionism and determinism which has conditioned much scientific thinking and which lies at the core of the scientific method may well be crucially flawed, and that the pursuit of AI represents the most recent, and potentially the most dangerous, *reductio ad absurdum* of that approach.

Cooley puts it thus:

> Central to the Western scientific methodology is the notion of predictability, repeatability and quantifiability. If something is unquantifiable we have to rarefy it away from reality, which leads to a dangerous level of abstraction.... Such techniques may be acceptable in narrow mathematical problems, but where much more complex considerations are involved, as in the field of design, they may give rise to questionable results. (Cooley, 1987, p. 53.)

Quoting Einstein, Cooley advances the view that imagination is far more important than knowledge, and that to draw a neat straight line divided off by little boxes is a false model of the way in which human expertise evolves:

> If an intelligent human being goes to a library to look up reference material, he or she will invariably be diverted off into a series of avenues which, in terms of the dedicated knowledge required, might be regarded as redundant. Yet the richness of human behaviour and human intelligence comes about as a result of these wide bands of knowledge and experience. (Cooley, 1987, p. 50.)

Although more concerned with the potential for damage of the inappropriate application of computer systems in the workplace, Cooley's recognition of the limitations of rule-based systems and their potential for downgrading and marginalizing human intelligence and expertise reads at times exactly like a critique of expert systems as such. Phrases like 'it is precisely that interaction between the objective and the subjective that is so important' (Cooley, 1987, p. 12), his conviction that experts 'are able to recognise whole scenes without decomposing them into their narrow features' (Cooley, 1987, p. 13), and his distrust of 'our overweening faith in science and in technological change' (Cooley, 1987, p. 8), can be mapped very precisely indeed on to the views of researchers into AI like Dreyfus.

In contrast to Papert's conception that the development of expertise represents a process of concretizing abstractions, Dreyfus proposes exactly the opposite contention, and employs his five-stage model of skill acquisition in order to demonstrate the point at which computer-based expert systems ceased to perform with any adequacy.

7.5   FROM NOVICE TO EXPERT

Dreyfus proposes five different levels of skill, which he places under the following headings:

(1) Novice
(2) Advanced beginner
(3) Competence
(4) Proficiency
(5) Expertise

A full account of these stages can be found in Dreyfus (1987). It is not necessary for us to explore each of these stages in detail, since a contrasting description of the novice and the expert will serve to highlight the two ends of the spectrum. First, the novice:

> The instruction process begins with the instructor's decomposing
> the task environment into context-free features that the beginner
> can recognize without benefit of experience. (Dreyfus, 1987, p. 44.)

The techniques involved here are familiar to every language teacher involved in developing language-acquisition skills at the beginner's stage. We are all thoroughly conversant with the concept of isolating the learner from the huge complexities of natural language, drawing out certain simple features together with some related transformations of those features and teaching them as if they existed in a separate world, as it were. Only once the simplified material has been assimilated do we incorporate it into the rest of the knowledge acquired, and begin to reveal it in its full complexities.

Only when a significant number of such subsets of the language have been successfully acquired by the learner do we branch out gradually from such a model into more complex areas. The computer can also be 'taught' in such a fashion, using heuristically based rules. But as the learner moves through the five stages, rule-based learning yields place to a more holistic approach to problem solving, finally arriving at the level of expertise, at which 'the expert performer ... understands, acts, and learns from results without any conscious awareness of the process'. (Dreyfus, 1987, p. 49.)

Expertise, claims Dreyfus, cannot be comprehended in terms of facts and rules, it functions in a quite different manner. And if we are even to attempt to model expertise acquisition and application on the computer, we must first develop a satisfactory model of mind, and then of the way in which the expert functions, and that we are a very long way from achieving.

But, you may be tempted to argue, there are problem domains which have clearer rules and less rough edges, in every sense, than trying to build a dry-stone wall. Think, for example, of areas such as chess that we have mentioned earlier. Here the possibilities are by no means as enormous as they are with a pile of irregularly shaped stones, and the power of modern computers should surely be capable of coping with the task of searching out the best next move in a chess game. Again, what appears to be straightforward turns out to be nothing of the sort. Alty and Coombs quote the calculations of Haugeland:

> With a complex game such as chess it would not be possible to search the whole game tree.... A five-move look-ahead gives a quadrillion (10^{15}) of possibilities, and forty moves (an average game) gives 10^{120} possibilities. He points out that there have been fewer than 10^{80} seconds since the beginning of the universe. (Alty and Coombs, 1984, p. 80.)

This is the famous 'combinatorial explosion', and it clearly requires some kind of tactical and strategic thinking to overcome the problem, since otherwise even human beings would be incapable of playing chess, even given the supposed enormously powerful parallel-processing power of the human brain.

This is the level of 'expertise' at which the computer has proven most successful, in closed problem domains with context-free rules, which can be mastered quite adequately by the use of heuristical techniques rather than deterministic programming. Although chess is a non-deterministic problem domain, where choices on the balance of probabilities have to be made, not decisions on the basis of certainties, it is possible to devise a chess-playing program of considerable power, up to the level of national champions and maybe higher.

Is there a middle way in this polarized debate? In his thoughtful evaluation of AI, Partridge seems to believe that there may well be an alternative to the starkly opposed views I have just outlined. He argues thus:

> Intelligence is widely believed to be the product of evolution and hence it is reassuring to know that it is perhaps likely to be decomposable into a modular hierarchy. But although we thus have some reason to hope that intelligence is a modular phenomenon, we still have to find the modules. (Partridge, 1986, p. 37.)

One way round the problem of knowledge engineering, of transferring human expertise to the computer, which has been proposed is to build a natural language interface which will enable the expert to talk directly to the computer without the intervention of the knowledge engineer. That, however, begs a rather large number of questions. Another alternative is to dispense with the process altogether, and replace it with a computer-based system which would:

> sever the umbilicus entirely: eliminate the knowledge engineer and the human expert, expose the program to the environment, and let it discover new knowledge on its own. (Lenat, 1983, p. 352.)

That is an option which, on the face of it, seems less than plausible, but it is an option which we shall be considering in the next chapter.

7.6   CONCLUSION

Expert systems, then, indicate a possible way forward for AI-like CALL, but at the same time it is clear that the difficulties are considerable. There is, as might be expected, an inverse correlation between the complexity, open-endedness, and exposure to real life of the field chosen and the success of the expert system which has been devised to cope with it.

There is another danger in applying this kind of approach and that is that there is really no such thing as an 'expert system', one single model which can be applied to all problem domains. There are only expert systems. By this I mean that the skills required for constructing an expert system cannot be transported lock, stock and barrel from one problem domain to another. It seems that all aspects of an expert system, with the exception of general principles, such as production rules, forward or backward reasoning, probability factors, and so forth, have to be invented anew for each problem domain.

As we have seen, the skills of the expert differ radically from one problem domain to another. I fear that a simplistic approach to an extremely complex area will have exactly the same kind of implications as Cooley observes in the area of industrial retraining, and for very similar reasons, in which he castigates 'this new moribund layer of "trainers"':

> Some of the ones I have encountered seem to believe that if you've trained a Labrador to retrieve you can also train a nuclear physicist... it is, after all, just training. (Cooley, 1987, p. 67.)

In addition, it should be remembered that the kind of expert systems we have seen are very restricted indeed in their potential, and that there is as yet little sign that genuine progress, scaling up, or whatever, is on the brink of taking place:

> If there existed a genuine capability for processing totally unformatted natural language data, it would be shouted from the rooftops — nobody (but an occasional publicity person) is shouting. (Garvin, 1985, p. 222.)

Clearly we shall have to be in the business not of writing programs of varying degrees of complexity to manipulate rigidly determined data, but of coping with a situation in which data is to a greater or lesser extent in the driving seat in determining what happens next. The difficulty that presents itself is one of finding a problem domain in which we can seek to operate such a system which is both meaningful and robust enough for the CALL environment.

8

From theory into practice

8.1 INTRODUCTION

In this chapter, I turn to consider to what extent it seems possible to translate the idea of AI-type CALL into practice, to discover how far we have come from the less than optimistic words of Geens, who wrote in 1981:

> Naive users may assume that the entire language teaching process can easily be automated and that the CAI may soon replace teachers. A more realistic assessment of the future suggests that CAI systems cannot do much more than automate the routine and predictable parts of foreign language teaching. Such systems, imaginatively employed, can free teachers for the necessarily open-ended dialogues that motivate students and help them achieve fluency in the language. (Geens, 1981, p. 46.)

I would concur with that statement to the extent that I regard it still as perfectly respectable and worthwhile to undertake work in first-generation CALL, as long as that work does not consist in reinventing the wheel. There is still a great deal to be achieved in that field, and I am constantly being pleasantly surprised by the ingenuity and skill demonstrated by the best practice. Even if and when a more advanced kind of AI-like CALL is realized, there will still be room for conventional software projects based on a less ambitious approach to the technology.

8.2 WHO PROGRAMS?

A number of important issues need to be faced in relation to attempts at taking CALL forward from its present impasse. The first question is one that I tackled earlier in relation to humanities computing generally and, by implication, to CALL also. That relates to the key issue as to who is to write this new generation of programs. Surely, the argument may go, the techniques required are such that they extend far beyond the competence of the average languages teacher.

The first point to recognize is that, of course, there were a large number of pretty amateurish attempts at CALL programming in the early days, and doubtless we shall continue to be embarrassed by the inadequacies of certain packages. However, those early days of CALL were an essential prelude to the later, more professional level of programming which is the norm today. The pioneers had to test the water to see if it was practical or possible to employ this new piece of technology at all in language teaching.

Secondly, although some academics may disapprove of the notion, there is no compulsory set of qualifications required for anyone to become a competent — even professional — programmer, and I am convinced that language teachers and students are uniquely qualified, by their understanding of natural language, to become programmers. I am sure others have shared my experience of seeing graduates and students with doctorates who have become involved in computing during their studies seeking and gaining employment as programmers, and it is equally true that many employers go in search of language and humanities graduates generally to train for programming.

I have frequently heard it asserted that, of course, a humanist cannot become a 'proper' programmer, since he lacks the necessary background, but I have not heard similar voices raised against some of the less than adequate efforts of scientific colleagues in a whole range of disciplines whose software I have examined and evaluated.

In my estimation, not only is there no barrier to a linguist becoming his own programmer at the AI level, I feel it would be even more undesirable at this phase to separate the programming from the project development, not least because the conventional notion of a deterministic program running a fixed set of data is no longer relevant. Data and program will become more and more interconnected, and as we have seen in our exploration of AI programs, there will be many cases where the data itself takes the leading role.

There is no need for linguists, then, to be defensive, although it is more than understandable that one of the pioneers of CALL, Farrington, should feel it necessary to express himself in these terms (his reference to Self is to Self, 1985, Chapter 19):

> A word should be said in defence, and in praise, of the DIY teacher–programmer, whom, I suspect, it will soon be fashionable to look down on. Now, it is certainly true that there is plenty of poor quality CALL material about, though it is interesting to note that none of Self's examples arc taken from the field of foreign language learning. ... If the next general of CALL materials does take off, it will depend upon the existence of a body of computerate language teachers. (Farrington, 1989, pp. 69–70.)

Having said that, it is more than likely that, given the complexity of such projects, the current trend towards group rather than individual projects will increase, with some members having a computing background, others with a chiefly linguistic competence. But there should be no rigid barriers between the two, and it is essential for programmers to become fully acquainted with the work of the linguists in the team, and vice versa.

8.3   WHAT KIND OF PROJECT?

The same constraints apply to AI CALL programs as to more conventional approaches. Nyns is quite right to remind us:

> Instead of setting out from the question 'What can I teach with my computer?' as too many CALL software developers seem to, the first question becomes 'Which media is best suited to teach such and such a skill?' (Nyns, 1988, p. 237.)

Of course, such a stance should not be taken so far as to place an absolute prohibition on working outwards from the technology to the learner, rather than the other way round. However, we should not allow ourselves to lose sight of the fact that while the early CALL experiments were within the context of a tried and tested computing environment, AI is still an aspiration rather than an achievement, and should be applied with considerable caution in real learning situations.

8.4   WHAT PROGRAMMING LANGUAGE?

One of the crucial questions to be asked at this junction is: what computing language should be used for the new era in CALL?

This is an extremely contentious area, and one in which I am sure that the conclusions which I reach will not be greeted with universal applause. The real problem, I feel, is that too many computer programmers are 'language-oriented', each with their own favourite programming language which they will defend against all comers with all the ferocity of a robin protecting its territory.

The issues are all the more complex now that a shift appears to be increasing away from procedural languages to declarative languages, and there is a parallel increase in emphasis on data rather than on the code itself.

There is a strong tide flowing against BASIC as a programming medium, although some of the opinion is based on misinformation:

> Modern versions of BASIC generally have quite sophisticated built-in graphics facilities. However, in natural language applications data structures are most important, and to my knowledge BASIC affords little else than arrays in that line. (Nyns, 1988, p. 238.)

The data structures of Mallard BASIC alone give the lie to the above assertion. Hall quotes Dijkstra as claiming that exposure to BASIC is disastrous for potential 'good' programmers, since 'they are mentally mutilated beyond any hope of regeneration'. She goes on to comment:

> While some may consider this statement rather extreme, the weight of judgment by the most eminent of people against using BASIC at all to teach programming is quite overwhelming. (Hall, 1987, p. 85.)

That assertion would be a little more impressive if the first name cited in its support had been more convincing to me than that of Papert.

The original designers of BASIC, Kemeny and Kurtz, claim that 'from its beginning, BASIC was developed according to carefully chosen philosophical principles'. (Kemeny and Kurtz, 1985, p. v.) They claim that what became known as 'street BASIC' tarnished the name and reputation of a potentially powerful and structured language, and indeed the subtitle of their new version of the language, True BASIC, runs: 'The structured language system for the future'. Modern dialects like True BASIC and Borland's Turbo BASIC, which eschew line numbers, are compiled and are highly structured, are surely — *pace* the prejudices or professional computer scientists — as capable of inculcating good programming practice as Pascal, COMAL, or any other language popular in the computing classroom.

Furthermore, as most language teachers have progressed from BBC BASIC, there is no reason why they cannot become advanced programmers in one of the modern versions of BASIC. I remain unimpressed by the strictures levelled against the language — or indeed, any particular language, by those who have a vested interest in promoting their own favourite language.

The case has been argued strongly that LISP or PROLOG are the inevitable languages for AI in the future, since they are declarative in mode rather than procedural, and handle data in special ways. Whilst recognizing that they are potentially much more impressive in dealing with certain kinds of data in particular ways, I am not convinced that it is a safe path to pursue to commit your research effort to an individual language which encourages you into a fairly restricted mould of thinking.

This implies that the kind of language which should be adopted would be a powerful, portable, general-purpose language. A few years ago the candidate would probably have been either APL or ALGOL 68, but neither has been taken up with great enthusiasm, which renders portability an insuperable problem. The current choice, then, is the language C, which is becoming increasingly recognized for its power and portability. The work of Johnston, described later in this chapter, is written in C in an area which hitherto might have been regarded as the exclusive province of LISP or PROLOG. For a thorough account of LISP, see Hasemer (1984). The standard work on PROLOG is Clocksin and Mellish (1981).

I am increasingly wary of those who claim that this or that language is the only way forward for any kind of programming, and for two reasons. The first is that current advances are threatening to render some special-purpose languages obsolete. For example, the transputer, if it makes an impact in CALL, and I suspect that it will sooner or later, will require a special kind of programming, not least because it has a parallel-processing language, occam, designed specially to drive it. (See Sharp, 1987, and Inmos, 1988.)

Secondly, my own view is that AI programming for CALL — and indeed, any programming activity — should be regarded as problem-based, not language-based. In other words, it is less than advisable to opt for a programming language which either restricts your line of enquiry or encourages you to explore one particular technique at the risk of excluding others. For this reason alone, I favour general-purpose languages, rather than languages like LISP or PROLOG, for precisely the reason that they have built into them certain kinds of concepts which, although currently in vogue, may well become an irrelevance when the next technological leap forward takes place.

It is also important to be flexible, never to be wedded to one language to the exclusion of all others. In future systems, for example, the prime requirement may well have nothing to do with list processing or representing a restricted subset of logical formulae, but with parallelism and distributed processing, for which some of the concepts associated with occam may well prove essential, and which indeed may well be assimilated into existing conventional programming languages.

In addition, I suspect that future developments may well enable us not just to select the programming environment, but to put together our own hardware suited to particular tasks. The age of designer hardware has yet to dawn, but I envisage a situation in which we can more or less acquire a bespoke computing environment suited to particular needs. Whether that comes in the form of literally different computers for different people, or a virtual system which can be configured for each particular need, is a matter for conjecture.

In the meantime, I believe it would be foolish in the extreme to argue that one programming language or another, or indeed, any one particular system environment, can claim the exclusive rights as the best or even the only way forward for AI and CALL.

8.5 OFF-THE-PEG

Much conventional CALL exists in the form of no-code authoring packages, templates for tutorial systems, testing inferencing ability, and much more besides.

AI authoring systems seem at first sight to be an impossibility, given the closer relationship between data and program, but there are some signs that it is possible to experiment on a small scale with what are regarded as AI packages. For example, VP Expert is one among a number of expert-system shells which enable the microcomputer user to experiment with rule-based systems, although it is by no means a true AI product.

In general terms, though, the possibilities of generating template programs or authoring packages are severely restricted the more AI-like the programming exercise becomes, as I have made clear in these pages. So the off-the-peg option is likely to be a very restricted option indeed.

8.6 CURRENT PROJECTS

The work underway in the field of CALL which aspires beyond the conventional approach of 'dumb' deterministic programs lays stress on working within a limited area, and on both the difficulties that lie in the path of progress and the need for the program to have knowledge of various kinds.

Ferney, in his description of work on small knowledge-based programs, makes as one of the cornerstones of his investigations the following principle, which is close to that of the experiments that I have made, which are described a little later in this chapter:

> It would therefore seem profitable for CALL programmers to direct their attention at modelling the *competence* of the human experts as well as simply 'canning' time after time the fruits of their experience. If such modelling could be achieved, or even partially achieved, then programs would *themselves* be able to generate and solve the very problems they set students. (Ferney, 1989, p. 18.)

In addition, he envisages the need for a tutor module (part of the program which 'knows' how to teach the material) and a student module, which 'knows' about the student's current capabilities.

In his search for what he calls 'local intelligence', he describes a mini-expert system for French nouns which is designed to:

> help advanced learners, who already possess a significant vocabulary, master the apparently arbitrary gender classification system of the nouns they already know. (Ferney, 1989, p. 29.)

The package, GENDER MENDER, is able to predict the gender of two out of three French nouns, partly by inbuilt rules, partly by a list of exceptions to those rules. The experience of this package has underpinned Ferney's conviction that:

> We need to concentrate instead on writing programs which contain an internal representation in executable form of the knowledge they seek to impart to the student. (Ferney, 1989, p. 24.)

In other words, the programs should in some sense be aware of what they are doing, and of the limits of their competence.

In similar vein, Gallerly and others have embarked on a 'semi-intelligent' syntax checker for French, which seeks to tackle the issue of the syntactic accuracy of French sentences (Gallerly and Butcher, 1989).

These and other projects indicate a movement away from deterministic CALL towards a more open-ended situation in which knowledge of various kinds plays a central role, and it is evident that the expert system in some guise or other is the main contender for seeking to push CALL in the direction of AI. So I turn now to consider in some detail two ways of implementing, to some extent at least, the concepts of the expert system in CALL.

8.7 GIBBER

The package designed by Johnston and described in his PhD thesis (Johnston, 1989) has been given a neat anti-acronym. The name GIBBER stands for German Interactive Binding Based Enquiry and Response program. It is, in a sense, a micro-world package in that it can cope with a restricted subset of declarative utterances, but it does try to push the technique of grammatical analysis to the limit. It is not so much a stand-alone system as a server module which analyses learner responses:

> GIBBER aims to provide a linguistically-based analysis of German text. The package's function is to analyse some learner input and to evaluate its syntactic correctness and semantic plausibility. Having identified (what it thinks is) an error, the package should be able to take a variety of actions, either to correct the error itself in certain circumstances ..., or to signal that an error has been detected. GIBBER effectively acts as a subroutine to a host CALL program, the host program passing GIBBER some learner input for processing. The package can then analyse the input to see how well it conforms with the model answer expected by the host CALL program. (Johnston, 1989, p. 158.)

The specification of the package was such that it should be capable of detecting a variety of syntactic errors, such as wrong usage of genders or plurals in nouns, wrong usage of grammatical cases, wrong declension of verbs, wrong usage of verbal auxiliaries, and wrong word order. In addition, it was also to be designed to cope with a certain subset of semantic errors, including both contradictory statements and inappropriate subject and verbs (such as 'The old man is young', and 'They eat water').

As Johnston rightly indicates, this kind of package would be involved in time-critical interaction with a learner, and he therefore designed it to be as efficient in terms of speed and memory requirement as possible. Significantly, he rejected either LISP or PROLOG, because of their heavy demands on memory caused by their recursive nature. For these reasons, Johnston determined on C as an ideal compromise between the speed and efficiency of assembler and the clarity of a high-level language. One might add to the advantages of C that it is a far more portable language than either LISP or PROLOG.

The technique which he adopts for the analysis of a noun cluster, for example, is to consider the possible forms permissible for each of the members of that cluster, and then to determine from that point either what the grammatical role of the form was or if it was syntactically incorrect. The example he offers is:

> der alte Mann

in the case of which there are six different possible interpretations of 'der', five of 'alte', and three of 'Mann'. Put them all together, and in this case just one possible correct solution emerges, that of nominative singular. Of course, the learner could have been taking a hopelessly wide swing at 'der alten Männer', the genitive plural form, but that error should be picked up at a later stage when the verb is analysed for singular or plural form, or even later when the host program matches the results provided by GIBBER with the model response.

In the morphological processing phase, Johnston employs an adapted form of the UNIX concept of the regular expression. This is a concept used by the file name matching command grep, and enables the user to employ a far more sophisticated variation on the wild card concepts of ? and * to be found in CP/M, MSDOS, and other operating systems. The chief advantage of the UNIX regular expression is that it permits you to search for alternatives, a range of characters, or strings not containing specified characters. Here are three illustrative examples from Waite *et al.* (1987, pp. 320ff), in which a fuller description can be found:

[wW]easel
[m-t]ap
[^m-t]ap

The first matches Weasel or weasel (not wWeasel). This means that the square brackets specify the bounds of the options. In the first case, any one of the characters can be substituted. In the second case, any of the range m–t can be accepted, from map to tap, and in the final example, any excluding the range m–t are acceptable.

Johnston ingeniously applies this concept to, for example, a very efficient means of storing the alternative vowels in the strong verb 'helfen':

h[eiao]lf

And he adapts the technique for the more complex cases where consonantal changes also occur. Equally, the dictionary of nouns is subjected to this UNIX-like treatment, where the forms of 'Mann' would be stored as this stem:

M[aä]nn

The analysis of the ending for correctness is left to a later stage.

Further refinements permit the recognition of separable prefixes, the use of auxiliaries, and adjectival forms.

Moving to semantic information, the dictionary entries for nouns, verbs and adjectives have information about their semantic valency tagged to them:

Each of these items is treated as an array of 32 bits, with a bit being set to on if the word belongs to the particular semantic category for that bit, or if the verb requires the particular syntactic slot for that bit. (Johnston, 1989, p. 172.)

So the techniques applied are designed to convert the natural language sentence into an internal representation, which he calls descriptors, to which bit masking techniques can be applied to ask questions relating to gender, case, whether it is a verb requiring the dative, and so forth.

Having determined the grammatical correctness or otherwise of the parts of the sentence and the sentence as a whole, the package then considers whether it makes semantic sense. For example, a verb may require a human subject and a concrete object, so that:

Das Mädchen schreibt das Buch

can be correctly disambiguated (since both nouns could be nominative or accusative) as 'The girl writes the book' and not the other way round. Word order is also checked for accuracy.

Although this program does not even lay claim to be a real intelligent substitute teacher, it does represent in my estimation a considerable step forward in the way in which CALL can function in a real teaching situation, and if the creators of MYCIN and R1 can call their products intelligent, then GIBBER too can lay some claims in that direction. Interestingly, it is an extension of traditional CALL into new areas rather than a rejection out of hand of the first-generation material from which it has evolved naturally.

8.8   THE INEXPERT SYSTEM

My own work in this field has equally concerned itself with the German sentence, but my objectives have been quite different from those of Johnston. Started on a BBC micro in the days when it seemed the only logical host machine for CALL material, but subsequently transferred to the less restrictive environment of the PC, the package (which was designed purely for research purposes and is as yet unbaptized) is based on the concept of creating a program which possesses some techniques for determining the constituent elements of a particular kind of declarative utterance, and, while having no knowledge at all, has the ability to acquire that knowledge; and then to try and teach it to understand sentences and to make guesses about new information on the basis of what it had learned already.

When the package arrives at a certain level of knowledge, it would then be appropriate to use it to teach learners of a given level of linguistic skills in a quite new fashion.

Let me explain what I am attempting to do by means of an illustration:

Der ältere Bruder meines Freundes überreicht seinem alten Vater
das nötige Geld.

That is a sentence typical of the kind which I have been 'teaching' my program to cope with. It concerns verbs which require an accusative object, usually a concrete noun, together with a dative indirect object, usually a human being or animate object. I chose sentences of this complexity level in order to discover what variations on the theme were 'understood' by the program without further modification.

The first task is to find the verb — or at least the main finite verb (past participles, separable prefixes and the like are dealt with at a later stage). In German this task is facilitated by the fact that it is located in the sentence as 'second idea', rather than shunted along as in English ('Yesterday we *went* to the zoo', in German: 'Gestern *gingen* wir ins Zoo').

It may be argued that, in the sentence quoted above, this is not the best first choice, since the 'first idea' is a long nominal cluster ('der ältere Bruder meines Freundes'), but the intention was to try and cope with finding what I regard as the syntactic and semantic linchpin of the sentence first, even if there are some problems to be overcome on the way. Also, this is the strategy which I want the learner to adopt when the program has learned enough itself to be released for teaching purposes.

Given the fact that, in German, nouns are capitalized, we have an added bonus to aid us in our search, and having taught the program to look for the first word in the sentence not beginning with a capital and testing its candidacy as the verb, stage one in the analysis of our sentence goes like this:

'meines' — possible verb. Not the verb: form of 'mein'

This is the kind of output that the program generates, since I am also concerned that the program explains what it is doing, partly to test whether I am succeeding in making it function properly, and partly too so that, when it is released to the learner, it can explain to them why it comes to particular conclusions.

After the failed candidacy of 'meines', the program latches on to 'überreicht', and then scans its verb list in the knowledge base. If it has not seen the verb before, it confesses its ignorance, but then tries to make some guesses about the verb based on its experience of other sentences which it has been fed. It is, of course, important to present the package first with common forms and standard sentences, a reasonable representation of the range of 'normal' material, in the same way as one does to the human learner, otherwise it could emerge with strange notions as to in what categories new forms might fall.

Let us assume, then, that the package has not been fed any sentences with the 'ihr' form of the verb. It can then inform us that there is a high probability that the verb is singular, present, third person. The programmer then confirms or corrects that supposition, and then answers a number of questions including the meaning of the verb, the kind of valency of subject, object (if there is one), and indirect object (again if there is one), and so on.

Now the program knows that it is looking for a singular subject which is human. It finds 'Bruder', and again let us assume that it has not come across this form before. It can tell us three things about 'Bruder' from the information before it, namely, that it is masculine, singular, and human. If it has not encountered 'Bruder' before, the program is clearly at an early stage of learning, and when it scans its database for similar forms, it may only come up with 'Vater'. On the basis of that information, it can offer the supposition that there is a high probability that the noun 'Bruder' forms its plural without adding 'e', 'en', or any other form, but that the central vowel will modify.

At a later stage of learning, the program copes more happily with a sentence like this:

Das junge Mädchen hat ihrer Schwester eine Ohrfeige gegeben.

Having found 'hat', the program knows that it is dealing with an auxiliary (full details of the auxiliaries are preprogrammed into the database), and checks for a participial form at the end of the clause. Then it comes back with the information that this is the perfect tense, third person singular, of the strong verb 'geben', which it has met before, and the information which it has about 'geben' is listed.

Now the program goes in search of a human subject, and so the process continues. The program will also offer examples from previous sentences it has met, so that it can inform you that 'schön' has also been associated with 'Mädchen'.

The program can also try and translate the sentence into English, and can generate syntactically correct and semantically meaningful sentences in English or German from the information it possesses which the learner can then either interrogate or translate.

The objective of the package, which is still in its developmental phase, is to provide a multipurpose resource which can be applied in a wide variety of different ways. It can be employed as a simple look-up dictionary, which can be taught new words, it can be asked to provide examples of a particular word in use — in fact, the range of applications is considerable.

The one application, though, which I am most interested to implement is that of allowing the learner to type sentences of a given range into the program, and watch the program try and make sense of them. This is an interactive and collaborative process which casts the learner in a more positive role, but which after each session will require careful checking by the teacher to ensure that incorrect information has not been keyed into the system.

In addition, I am seeking to move the weight of emphasis away from facts and information and their correct aquisition to a greater stress on techniques and processes. I hope that my inexpert system, when interacting with a learner, will demonstrate by the correct and inaccurate guesses it makes what kind of processes a computerized 'learner' goes through and how similar they are to the mixture of insights and brick walls which the human user of the program encounters. By so doing, the hope is that it will sharpen the learner's techniques for coping with unfamiliar material and for manipulating material which is already familiar.

The reader will have noticed that I have refrained from using the term 'AI-type CALL' in relation to this package. There will be those who would be sorely tempted to regard this kind of program as a great leap forward into AI. I tend to be considerably more cautious. All I am seeking to do is to recognize the severe problems involved in trying to implement expert systems in a CALL environment, and to stand the expert system on its head, as it were, at a point on the learning scale at which we are dealing with situations which are above the novice level, certainly, but which are not at expert level.

I do not have any illusions that it is possible or practical to 'scale up' the program to an expert level of knowledge of open-ended input. But I am convinced that this kind of application, the move towards the sentence level, which is a common theme in 'new-generation' CALL, as I might name it, is the most practical way of moving CALL further up the learning scale, as it were, away from drill and practice into a more exciting and challenging role, which is still within the bounds of practicality for the teacher and learner in real situations.

In the meantime, we should keep a watching brief on developments in the field of AI to determine whether any of the actual advancements that take place (rather than the flood of predications which engulf the popular media) can have a beneficial role to play in this difficult but worthwhile field.

8.9 CONCLUSION

In a real sense, we are still at the kind of impasse I described in relation to the early days of humanities computing. Then, the concordance process 'simply' consisted of taking a text, sorting the words into alphabetical order, and then listing them in context.

Some of the difficulties lurking in that glib description of the concording process are not relevant to our present discussion: unlike medieval German, for example, we are not concerned about the integrity of the text. Nor is the problem of sorting into alphabetical order a particularly critical one. But we still face the problem of the word as a less than adequate parallel to the sense unit which we seek to identify. A word can either be less than, or indeed more than, a single sense unit, and in German in particular, the words that constitute a sense unit are not necessarily adjacent in a sentence. That holds good particularly in the case of separable verbs and compound tenses in main clauses.

The problem which has become the most substantial is that of the context. In the concordance, we are simply seeking some rough and ready compromise between creating piles of output and smothering the message in data on the one hand and, on the other, printing out a context so tight that it does not invariably yield up the full sense of the current keyword.

In AI-type work, however, the 'context' can reach far beyond the physical text on the page, and indeed it typically does imply a knowledge of the cultural, political, physical and many other kinds of contextual environment, without which the text cannot be properly interpreted.

So we are still struggling on the dividing line between what can be quantified and what cannot, but now the difficulties have been compounded by the quest for understanding the text in a programmable fashion. How this impasse is to be resolved, if indeed it can be resolved, is currently far from clear. Perhaps we shall one day be capable of generating 'true' AI-based CALL, but then I fear that we shall be moving away from the puzzling richness of natural language to a normatized, sanitized form of the language, in which by then it will not be necessary for us to bother to master a foreign tongue. The all-powerful computer will do it for us, and there will be one less skill for us to master, one less pleasure in intellectual achievement to record.

If you take the aspirations of the AI evangelists *ad absurdum*, as it were, this is where it inevitably leads — to the machine taking over the necessity for us to learn about other cultures and languages, to our intellectual diminishment and to the marginalization of human skills in yet another field.

9

Recent developments

9.1 INTRODUCTION

When I first embarked on this book some four years or so ago, my principal objective was to consider the potentiality and desirability of the implementation of what might be termed 'classical' AI in relation to CALL.

Leaving aside the fact that my initial enthusiasm rapidly cooled, it soon came to my attention that AI-related CALL, if it was to be introduced, would not inevitably come by one of the routes which mainstream AI researchers have so far pursued.

At that time, CALL was perceived almost exclusively in terms of an interaction between the learner on the one hand and a desktop microcomputer on the other. In other words, the constituent elements of the interaction were as follows:

Student, using — eyes
                — keyboard skills
Computer, using — screen

This had been the set of parameters within which my first experimentations with CALL were conducted, although instead of a colour screen, I had to operate with the less-satisfactory environment of a clattering teletype, which clearly had little to offer in terms of attractive layout, or even lower-case characters, let alone diacritics and exotic character sets.

As the main thrust of AI concentrated on that kind of interaction, it seemed inevitable to follow a similar upgrade path, as it were, for AI-based CALL; that is to say, a certain level of keyboard skills forming the student's input route to the computer, and a visual display constituting the responding sensory path from computer back to student.

Within those limitations, as I hope I have demonstrated, a great deal can be achieved, and I suspect much more is waiting to be done, since even the latest collection of papers on CALL (Cameron, 1989), which appeared as I was putting the finishing touches to this book, refers only in passing to other elements than the keyboard and screen in the CALL process.

9.2   COMPUTER-CONTROLLED CASSETTE RECORDER

The first additional approach to the HCI in CALL which I encountered came with the computer-controlled cassette recorder manufactured by Tandberg (the TCCR), with which I was involved in the concept design and controller software.

This device was a cassette recorder with a digital clock controlled by an on-board 2K ROM chip, controllable either from the usual cassette keys (play, stop, fast forward, and so on), or via the RS232 port directly by a computer. Using appropriate software, it is possible to emulate not just the standard controls of the recorder, but also additional commands with feedback from the recorder.

For example, it is possible to request the recorder to fast forward to 3 minutes 10 seconds, then play until 3 minutes 20 seconds. Given the problems of tape stretch and other technical difficulties with timing-based instructions, the command set was enhanced to cope with a situation in which the computer can request the recorder to play until three seconds' silence occurs, and then to move forward to the beginning of the next set of sounds.

This instruction set gave a powerful added impetus to the potential of conventional CALL. Using the system, I devised a dictation program, incorporating its own authoring system, which represents a considerable advance in the capabilities of CALL. It was simply necessary for the teacher to speak the dictation in the normal way.

The teacher first types into a file on screen the correct answer in full, split up into the sections into which he or she will divide the text when speaking it at dictation speed. Then there comes a straight read through of the text, then a read through with gaps, during which time the learner keys in the response on the screen. The recorder is then wound back to the beginning and the first read through is repeated. Finally, the computer marks the result on screen or records the outcome for the teacher to mark (or both).

The most significant advance which this represents on the conventional dictation was that the learner was no longer forced into a straitjacket of having the sequence of events determined for the whole class in advance. If the program's parameters are set up to permit it, the learner can request the program to re-read a given part of the dictation, so that a misheard word or difficult spelling can be tried again and again, once more within limits set in advance by the teacher.

Such text can be marked 'interactively' by the program. The technique I adapted was to mark with an up-arrow the point on the line at which the learner began to go astray.

Finally, and most importantly, it is all very well for a learner to be told that they are wrong; what is necessary is for the error to be explained and a strategy for overcoming it spelled out. In any dictation situation, the teacher is usually setting out to test particular spelling problems which the learner is supposed to be beginning to cope with at this stage of the language-acquisition process. A facility was therefore built into the program to interrogate the learner's completed response and to cause the cassette recorder to play certain subsequent sections of tape dependent upon given conditions.

If, for example, a learner had failed to type 'je parlais' but had ended the verb with a 't', a not uncommon error, then if it occurred a reinforcing message can be read out from the tape. This reinforcement phase turned out to be the most powerful feature of the program as a whole, and enabled the teacher to input selective advice which directly met the needs of individual learners. Of course, sections of the tape could also be read out unconditionally to all learners if that was deemed appropriate.

In this respect, one criticism of the 'inflexibility' and lack of responsiveness of CALL was overcome, and it points to the fact that a considerable amount of progress in the direction of open-format responses to the learner can be made without taking a single step in the direction of AI-like techniques.

It was my former colleague Derek Lewis who confronted the more difficult challenge presented by the recorder, namely, of trying to deal with free-format input by the learner. In a program called RELIC, (REading and LIstening Comprehension) (Lewis, 1985), he devised a system which sought by various matching techniques in relation to predetermined responses to cope with a range of correct responses to a question testing the ability of the learner in either reading comprehension from the screen or in listening to the TCCR.

Thus, in response to a question such as 'In the passage, how did Columbus cross the Atlantic?' a range of correct responses can be allowed for in the model answer file, and certain unwanted responses (like 'by aeroplane') can be marked as unacceptable. Generalized fuzzy matching routines can also be incorporated under the control of the teacher. It is in many ways an experimental package bringing together computer and recorder, and Lewis points in the manual to the difficulties which lie in the path of those seeking to implement this kind of program:

> The specification of appropriate answers for open-ended text material is not easy. The package aims to provide a degree of flexibility and range beyond what is currently available in language learning software, but the teacher may still find that all possible linguistic variations for a valid answer are difficult to cover through sheer enumeration, even using the keyword or key phrase principle. He is therefore advised to consider carefully the kind of questions he is asking of the learner and to experiment on his own material with this in mind.

Once again, the familiar warning signs appear: restriction in range is a necessity, and it is clear that the degree of difficulty in moving rapidly towards open-ended responses rapidly reaches the point at which sheer cost-effectiveness considerations cause the experimenter to draw back, probably some time before the theoretical or practical limitations of the technique have been attained.

The above two experimental packages were targeted on the BBC micro. One further practical limitation which had to be borne in mind was the physical access time for the cassette recorder. To move more than a few seconds' play time, even given the high motor speed of the equipment, meant a pause readily detectable by the learner, which had to be kept within bounds if it was not to become unacceptable.

This rapidly came to be the case in a further experimental program which I wrote which sought to add to the conventional question and answer type of tutorial CALL audio input, both at the point of question and in selective reinforcement of the learner responses. The concept functioned well enough, but learners rapidly tired of having to wait even a few seconds before the response targeted on them was reached on the tape, and it rapidly became clear that the technology had its limitations as far as learner reaction was concerned. Now, with the promise of WORM technology for CD players, this time constraint may well be largely overcome, but, as stressed earlier, the TCCR serves to add one more response mode on the part of the computer rather than to extend CALL in the direction of AI.

9.3   SPEECH SYNTHESIS

There is, however, a technology which is becoming available which may overcome both the problem of time during which the learner is waiting for his response to come on-line, and also the considerable time input by the teacher in preparing the audio and computer-file based material for tests of this kind, and this is the speech synthesizer.

Perhaps the most sophisticated such equipment generally available comes bundled with the Amiga computer from Commodore, and I have been conducting a number of experiments with the Amiga 2000 to determine whether the technology has reached the stage at which it can be used 'live' in language teaching. The synthesizer is phonemically based, and employs the Arpanet sound representation system. The synthesizer is based on a Narrator Device which accepts a normal text string in English, converts the string into a phonemic string (with the aid of a translator library, but it 'has a go' at exception words directly), and then speaks the words through the loudspeakers.

Additionally, it can display mouth shapes on the screen corresponding to the sounds created. The speech output is understandable and would certainly, even unmodified, constitute a powerful aid to the visually handicapped. It is possible to vary the pitch, inflection, rate, type of voice, volume, and other parameters, and it clearly has potential as a language teaching tool, although its best quality is acceptable rather than outstandingly natural. For a technical description of the Narrator Device, see Mortimore (1987, vol. 2, pp. 91ff.), and the Amiga Basic manual (1985, pp. 8–132ff.).

But again, this is not a device to extend the range of CALL into AI. Like the TCCR, it is more an extension to the existing mode of CALL than a great leap forward into AI-related programming. Such devices forge the link between computer and language laboratory which gave the latter the potential for a new lease of life, but in essence they lack the necessary flexibility and power to be regarded as more than a useful adjunct to the 'look and type' interaction offered by the computer, and the 'listen and say' interaction in the language laboratory.

In the past couple of years, a number of new potential kinds of interaction with the computer have come on to the agenda, and it is important to consider them and the impact which they may well exert in AI generally and in CALL in particular.

These systems fall into two categories: software advances and hardware advances. The hardware advances are in the field of videodisc and compact disc, and in software, hypertext leads the way. First, we briefly consider laser- disc technology.

9.4 VIDEODISC AND CD

The Philips laservision system, initially aimed at the mass market, but failing to gain an impact because of the dominance of read–write cassette-based video systems, has evolved in the educational and technical spheres as a potentially very powerful interactive teaching medium. One researcher concludes a recent paper, though, with this note of warning:

> In working with interactive video, it is all too easy to be excited and misled by the sophistication of the hardware and by the obvious attractiveness of the medium. This must not, however, be allowed to obscure the crucial questions of whether or not it actually works. Interactive video is certainly exciting, but it is important to obtain an objective and sanguine assessment of its effectiveness. (Hill, 1987, p. 58.)

He goes on to stress, as I did earlier in this book, that the constraints of the marketplace can prevent the potential of the technology from being realized. Enough institutions must have the hardware if the appropriate software base is to be established. In addition, the substantial amount of time required in designing IV systems must be equally recognized and justified.

There is no doubt that a system which can hold over 50 000 frames of information, still or moving pictures, as well as analogue and digital data, with an optimum maximum search time of three seconds, when linked with a microcomputer-based CALL system, bears considerable promise.

But it is equally true that the wider consumer base of CD systems will encourage research into CD-ROM and CDI (compact disc as a read-only database and interactive compact disc), and this may well spell the end of the videodisc. This is especially so since just one CD is capable of storing 550 megabytes of information, and commercial databases, from lists of books in print to encyclopedias are all coming on stream to exploit the technology.

Clearly, new video and audio dimensions are available in these systems, but it is far from clear what their actual impact in CALL will be. A small number of pioneering studies are under way, but whether or not they will have a substantial impact on CALL is yet to be seen.

9.5   HYPERMEDIA

A handful of years ago, the concept of hypertext was virtually unknown. Now it threatens to become one of the great educational technology growth industries, one which will impinge considerably on AI-like applications in CALL, as well as in areas as diverse as business, industry and library systems. There are even suggestions that it might represent the next stage forward in the user interface beyond the 'windows' concept in contemporary microcomputer systems. It is an area which, although in its infancy, is of such importance that it merits careful consideration, not least because one can detect in it some of the more worrying aspects of the over-enthusiasm of researchers into AI generally.

A word of explanation is called for before we consider the past, potential, and limitations of the concept. Hypertext itself means 'non-sequential text'. The term hypermedia extends that notion to other forms of expression, such as video, graphics, and so forth. To examine the concept in a little more detail: most texts are, like the one you are reading now, designed to be linear and static. You start at the beginning and (I hope) read right through to the end. Your interaction with the text consists of assimilating the facts, and following the arguments and views I put forward until you have accumulated a total picture of my perception of the role of AI in CALL. And there the interaction ceases: you are not invited to take your own path through the book, to read page 45, then page 22, and then page 90. Nor are you invited either to add to or subtract from the existing contents of the book on the printed page. Of course, you may take notes or put a red pencil through my less cogent arguments, but none of those activities in any way changes the book itself.

It remains a static, one-way delivery system. A dictionary, on the other hand, although still a one-way system, is designed to be read in a non-sequential manner. You do not have to read all of a dictionary (indeed, it is hardly advisable to attempt to do so) from cover to cover in order to derive information from it. In its simplest form, hypertext on a computer system is rather like accessing a dictionary database, but with a number of significant differences. In a dictionary system, we approach the database with a particular enquiry. If that enquiry is initially satisfied — in other words, you find an entry for the word or phrase whose meaning you are seeking — then further non-sequential use of the database may be required if the entry contains a 'q.v.' or 'see . . .' reference to another entry or entries. In turn, those further referenced entries may themselves point you to other entries.

That mimics one aspect of hypertext. The individual entry is termed a *node*, which can be defined as the basic unit of information within the database, and which usually occupies no more than a single screenful of text (or graphics). Each individual entry is related more or less strongly to the other nodes in the database by means of *associative links* or pointers which invite you to take one or more paths from the current node to the next node.

The means by which you as the user of the hypertext system move through the system is known as *navigation*, and since one of the potentially most difficult aspects of using such packages is that of orientation, of finding out where you are in the system, there is a tool called a *browser*, which typically takes the form of a graphical representation on screen of where you have come from, where you are now, and what current options for onward movement you have.

This is not the place to explore in detail how such a system works, its strengths and its deficiencies, but it is appropriate to consider briefly how hypertext as a concept evolved in the first place.

The history of hypertext antedates the computer and has its roots in information science, most significantly in library information storage and retrieval systems. The real father of hypertext was Vannevar Bush, an electrical engineer who contributed significantly to the first electronic analogue computer (called the differential analyser), which itself was a direct antecedent of the modern electronic digital computer. Bush was also active in the field of scientific politics, in which he served on committees for President Roosevelt, and it was this combination of practical scientific work and involvement in the wider world of decision-making that gave him the breadth of vision to have a direct influence on the two principal researchers who brought the notions of hypertext to reality: Engelbart and Nelson.

In a seminal article written in 1945, entitled 'As we may think' (published in *Atlantic Monthly*), Bush proposed a system for information storage and retrieval called Memex, which was designed to seek to prevent the post-war explosion of scientific literature from becoming completely uncontrollable. Curiously, then, this wealth of scientific journal literature impacted upon two significant but quite distinct areas of AI — that of MT, in relation to the problems of translation, and now hypertext, in the context of the sheer volume of that knowledge.

However, it must be stressed that what Bush was seeking to achieve — in the same kind of way that the early MT researchers worked — was the automation of an essentially mechanical or clerical process, rather than a completely reworked and newly thought-out system appropriate to the power and potential of the new electronic equipment coming on stream.

The underlying concepts of Bush's work were taken up and extended by a worker from Stanford Research Institute, Douglas Engelbart. His concern was with using the computer as a kind of extension of the intellect of man, with its primary emphasis placed on the storage and access of information to be shared among a number of researchers. Called Augment, it 'stores information in a sophisticated hierarchical structure allowing non-hierarchical branching'. (Fiderio, 1988, p. 238.) Incidentally, it was Engelbart who actually invented the computer mouse as a means of maximizing speed of interaction between the user and his system.

The concepts of Engelbart were further extended by Ted Nelson, who was actually responsible for inventing the term hypertext. His vision of an interactive, ever-growing computerized knowledge environment was far grander than either Bush or Engelbart; his project Xanadu:

> will be an ever-expanding publishing environment that millions of people could use to create, interact, and interconnect with linked electronic documents and other forms of hypermedia. (Fiderio, 1988, p. 238.)

Hypertext first came into the public arena when the Apple computer company bundled with its Mac computers a hypertext program called HyperCard. It is a relatively straightforward implementation of hypertext concepts, but it does have the advantage of containing a series of scripts which can be written in a language with a syntax close to 'normal' English.

The other key event which focussed attention on hypertext was the conference Hypertext 87 at the University of North Carolina, Chapel Hill.

For an account of the history of hypertext, see Conklin (1987). A somewhat evangelistic description of hypermedia can be found in the pages of *Interactive multimedia* (Ambron, 1988). There is a special sequence of articles on hypertext, entitled 'A grand vision' in *Byte* magazine (October 1988), and the July 1988 edition of *Communications of the ACM* is devoted to the subject, and contains six of the papers delivered at Hypertext 87.

In a project to investigate the Oxford English Dictionary's electronic database as a means of exploring the problems inherent in hypertext, Raymond stresses the importance in current work of being able to construct the nodes in an appropriate form:

> Hypertext is typically characterised by small fragments of text interconnected by machine-supported links. Since most existing texts are not fragmented in this way, the key problem in converting them to hypertext is the development of text fragments and links. (Raymond, 1988 p. 871.)

Provided, of course, that this is an appropriate model for the future development, more powerful hypertext systems are in prospect. There are problems, too, of the integrity of data, but that is not the exclusive province of hypertext — ensuring that the database is comprehensive, updated, and above all accurate is a headache which besets any large information storage and retrieval exercise.

One of the key researchers in the field, Frank Halasz, joint creator of the Notecards system at Xerox, poses (Halasz, 1988) seven issues about the weaknesses of the current hypertext systems which must be resolved before meaningful progress can be made. In particular, he stresses that 'the current model needs to be extended beyond simple nodes and links', and argues in general terms that 'there is a great deal of difficult design and implementation to be done before hypermedia systems can achieve their potential'. (Halasz, 1988, p. 851.)

Hypertext has both considerable potentiality and holds dangers for the over-enthusiastic supporter of the concept. Yet again, the risk is present that the fallacy of the first successful step is alive and well and living in hypertext. In the words of a study of knowledge-management systems based on the hypermedia concept:

> The good news is that hypermedia designers can expect lifetime employment.... The bad news is that the rich design space for hypermedia presents designers with many agonising trade-offs.... Our experience with these trade-offs has encouraged us to practise a design philosophy of *voluntary simplicity*, striving to make do with fewer concepts and mechanisms. (Akscyn *et al.*, 1988, p. 834.)

Furthermore, despite some over-optimistic observations by its proponents, hypertext by itself is not cognate with AI; it simply represents an attempt at a more sophisticated approach to the concept of the structured interactive database.

9.6 CONCLUSION

It is clear, therefore, that new software techniques and technological advances have the potential to make radical changes to the AI agenda as far as CALL is concerned. What appears to be impossible now can become a reality because of some advance or other which has been made in what may at first sight appear to be a completely unrelated field. It is important for CALL researchers to maintain an awareness of the potential which such advances might bring to their own work.

Heather, in his informative account of the impact of laserdisc technology (both videodisc and CD) in the humanities, is quite right to underline this point:

> It is important for CAL practitioners to begin to think in terms of technology such as videodisc and CD-ROM. The question is not just one of avoiding the enthusiasm for re-inventing the wheel, though this is still a thriving occupation. There seems to be some tendency for those who enter the CAL field to remain within the horizons created the first time they switched on a microcomputer.... It cannot be denied of course that videodisc and CD-ROM are still expensive options, and are yet to be fully proved in the classroom. But if, as it is sometimes said, CAL has not really started yet, it is surely with such technology — together with artificial intelligence techniques — that CAL will move towards a more authentic role. (Heather, 1987, p. 53.)

Whilst I concur with those sentiments, it is evident that the new options we have considered in this chapter — videodisc, CD and hypertext in particular — are currently unwieldy options in their infancy, and that there is no clear evidence to support the view that any or all of them will bring about the promised breakthrough into real AI-based CALL.

Futurology is a dangerous game, but the lessons of the past, if they can be extrapolated into the future, indicate that it will be by the agency of some computing hardware breakthrough that a more sophisticated generation of CALL will come into being. Perhaps that breakthrough has already occurred in the shape of, say, Inmos's transputer with its parallel potentiality, and we have not yet recognized it. Or perhaps the breakthrough still lies in the future.

Of course, there is one kind of advance which has not been mentioned in this chapter, and that is radical progress in our understanding of how the human mind functions, whether the modularity of mind does indeed extend into every area of our subconscious thought processes, or whether there is some other form of structured functionality which can be emulated on present or future computing systems. I fear that without progress in this area, all the new technology the scientists can throw at us will be powerless to bring about genuine progress in AI-based CALL beyond a very limited range.

There seem, though, to be some hopeful indications in this sphere, with the increasing interdisciplinary interest in the concepts of chaos, complex systems, and notions such as strange attractors, period doubling, and other structures which have been recognized as having some kind of regularity despite their apparent amorphousness. Perhaps — or is this just idle speculation? — a 'butterfly effect', in which a small, apparently insignificant occurrence in an unrelated area impacts on a whole sphere of activities, similar to that observed by the students of chaos, will bring about a breakthrough in our understanding of the human mind.

10

Conclusion

The literature of AI is filled with confident promises of a new computing age in which intelligent machines will expand and extend the capabilities of human influence and control over the environment in ways of which we currently cannot conceive.

But what is becoming increasingly clear is that the creation of machine intelligence, if it ever came, would be much more like opening Pandora's Box than ushering in a new golden age. In recent years, the ardent advocation of the new technology of AI as proposed by enthusiasts like Marvin Minsky has been considerably tempered by voices of caution, which have argued not only that the aspirations of AI might not only be attainable, but that they may be thoroughly undesirable for a variety of reasons, which are not just theoretical in nature, but which impinge directly on AI in CALL.

As we have seen, cautious edging forward is in my estimation the only viable approach to the application of AI, not least because of the central issue of the robustness of a program which may be based on fuzzy matching, weak algorithms and seeking a passable rather than the one and only solution to a deterministic problem which can be spelled out in algorithmic terms. At no time must the learner be allowed to lose confidence in his electronic tutor, since otherwise the whole exercise is lost and the expenditure of time and effort wasted.

Given current technological limitations, it is clear that there is a point beyond which AI-based CALL cannot currently advance. Whether that point will more or less rapidly advance indefinitely until full-blooded AI has been achieved is a matter for speculation.

One area of concern which has not so far surfaced is the prospect not that the computer will enhance the learning of foreign languages, but may well replace it. The first step in the direction of the 'de-skilling' of the learning situation was the introduction of the electronic calculator, which has left a whole generation of schoolchildren with no necessity for learning tables. One recent advertisement for an electronic calculator did indeed carry the proud boast: 'Calculators so advanced they do the thinking for you'.

Children have lost a skill, but more importantly than that, they have forfeited the valuable learning processes which go along with it. Now technology takes over from brainpower in more and more areas of our lives, with a consequent and as yet unquantified knock-on effect on our intellectual and human growth and development. Perhaps the first equivalent stage for modern language learning will be the hand-held multilingual dictionary, and ultimately a translating machine which will remove from us the tiresome necessity of learning the language of another country at all.

Somewhere in the rush for technological advance the human factor is in danger of being overlooked. Elsewhere, in the business and industrial worlds, the dangers are far greater. People become subordinate to or are replaced by machines; the skills and interpersonal relationships which contribute so substantially to both human satisfaction and human identity are being directly challenged even by the technology currently available. Accounts of the threat to the office environment, such as those articulated by Zuboff (1988), and to the industrial workplace (Cooley, 1987) must be listened to and the positive alternatives which they propose heeded.

Most directly related to this book are the concerns raised in a collection of essays edited by Douglas Sloan (Sloan, 1984a) which offers, in the words of its subtitle, 'a critical perspective' on the role of the computer in education. Here, too, marginalization of the human learner is feared, in that the computer and the reductionist brand of thought which it encourages is emphasizing the mechanistic at the expense of the humane.

Sloan argues that the kind of imagery which we build up in school pupils is vital to their perception of the world as they grow and develop. He states his case in these words:

> Our images will eventually give us the kind of world we come to know through them. . . . If we persist in an exclusive preoccupation with mechanistic images, we will get a mechanical world. (Sloan, 1984b, p. 7.)

So I make no apologies for being excessively concerned with the theory behind the practice, not least in the field of expert systems where the main thrust for AI-type CALL is properly to be found. The scaling-up of micro worlds is a severe enough challenge, but matching that to a positive and robust environment for the learner is a problem which may well not be resolved within a decade:

> One of the problems is that no one knows how to make a satisfactory model of a domain such as commonsense physics, so no one can put into a program the physical intuitions a physics teacher uses. Likewise, and for exactly symmetrical reasons, no one is able to make a computer model of the everyday understanding the student brings to the learning task. (Dreyfus, 1987, p. 51.)

Also I fear for a world in which such expert systems are given real live problems to solve, with life and death decisions delegated to computing machinery. The human hospital consultant, like any expert, is not infallible. He walks the wards, makes his observations and diagnoses, and does his best at the current level of his expertise to preserve life and combat disease and disability. But he makes his mistakes and learns from them. Let us assume that we succeed in transplanting his expertise into the computer. Then we allow the role of the consultant to be taken over by the computer. The computer takes control. It decides who is to be operated on, and how.

Are we going to allow a piece of machinery to imitate human fallibility? In reply to the assertion that 'of course' we should design out human weaknesses from such a system, my question is: how does anyone propose that such an objective can be achieved, especially given the fact that humans cannot agree among themselves about courses of action to be taken within a complex problem domain? Because we are observing from a specific perspective, our conclusions will almost inevitably be different.

And there are the moral issues to consider, too. Without intending to be facetious, are we to build into our electronic consultant Roman Catholic views on abortion, or free-thinking views on euthanasia?

In going down this dangerous path, it seems to me that we are indeed seeking to marginalize humanity and create a race of computerized monsters which, when the power of decision-making is given into their hands, will decree that the human race, with its passions, inconsistencies, foibles and frailties, should be declared redundant, and that the intelligent machine shall inherit the earth.

And that, fundamentally, is why the initial enthusiasm which engendered this book has now turned so sour. My one consolation is that, without exception, the researchers in the field of CALL, particularly those seeking to implement AI-like programs, have demonstrated a singularly levelheaded approach to the problems concerned, and have no illusions about the scale of the challenge that lies before them. Perhaps there is a lesson here which we might tentatively offer to others engaged in this potentially dangerous endeavour.

Bibliography

Abbot, R. J. (1987) Knowledge abstracts *Comm. ACM*, **30** (No. 8), 664–671.

Adams, A., and Jones, E. (1983) *Teaching humanities in the electronic age.* Open University Press, Milton Keynes.

Adman, P. (1987) Computers and history. In: Rahtz, S. *Information technology in the humanities: tools techniques and applications.* Ellis Horwood, Chichester, pp. 92–103.

Ager, D. (1986) Help levels in CALL materials. In: Cameron, K. C., Dodd, W. S., and Rahtz, S. P. Q. (eds) *Computers and modern language studies*, Ellis Horwood, Chichester, pp. 100–112.

Ahmad, K., Corbett, G., Rogers, M., and Sussex, R. (1985) *Computers, language learning and language teaching.* CUP, Cambridge.

Airenti, G. and Bara, B. G. (1981) An intrasystemic approach to belief. In: Elithorn, A., and Banerji, R. (eds) *Artificial and human intelligence*, Elsevier, Amsterdam, pp. 265–269.

Akscyn, R. M., McCracken, D. L., and Yoder, E. A. (1988) KMS: a distributed hypermedia system for managing knowledge systems. *Comm. ACM*, **31** 820–835.

Allport, D. A. (1980) Patterns and actions: cognitive mechanisms are content-specific. In: Claxton, G. (ed.) *Cognitive psychology: new directions.* Routledge & Kegan Paul, London.

Alty, J. L. and Coombs, M. J. (1984) *Expert Systems Concepts and Examples.* NCC, Manchester.

Allwood, C. M. (1986) Novices on the computer: a review of the literature. *Int. J. Man–Machine Studies*, **25** 633–658.

Amarel, S. (1981) Expert behaviour and problem representations. In: Elithorn, A., and Banerji, R. (eds) *Artificial and human intelligence.* Elsevier, Amsterdam, pp. 1–41.

Amarel, S. (1983) Problems of representation in heuristic problem solving: related issues in the development of expert systems. In: Groner, R., Groner M., and Bischof, W. F. (eds) *Methods of heuristics.* Lawrence Erlbaum, London, pp. 245–350.

Ambron, S., and Hooper, K. (1988) *Interactive multimedia.* Microsoft/ Penguin, Harmondsworth.

Amiga Basic (1985) Amiga Basic Manual. Microsoft Corporation.

Bailey, R. W. (ed.) (1981) *Computing in the humanities. Papers from the fifth international conference on computing in the humanities, Ann Arbor, Michigan, May 1981.* North-Holland, Amsterdam.

Banerji, R. B. (1981) GPS and the psychology of the Rubik cubist: a study in reasoning about actions. In: Elithorn, A., and Banerji, R. (eds) *Artificial and human intelligence.* Elsevier, Amsterdam, pp. 67–79.

Bangs, P. (1987) Interactive video in language learning: the Thames Valley experience. In: Coleman, J. (ed.) *The interactive videodisc in language teaching.* Lochee Publications, New Alyth, Perthshire, pp. 103–112.

Barchan, J. (1986) New approaches to computer aided language learning. In: Cameron, K. C., Dodd, W. S. and Rahtz, S. P. Q. (eds) *Computers and modern language studies.* Ellis Horwood, Chichester, pp. 93–99.

Bar-Hillel, Y. (1960) The present status of automatic translation of languages. In: Alt, F. L. (ed.) *Advances in computers,* Academic Press, London, pp. 91–163.

Barstow, D. R. (1982). The roles of knowledge and deduction in algorithm design. In: Hayes, J. E., Michie, D., and Pao, Y.-H. (eds) *Machine intelligence 10.* Ellis Horwood, Chichester, pp. 361–381.

Begeman, M. L. and Conklin, J. (1988) The right tool for the job. *Byte Magazine* October 1988, 255–266.

Bender, T. K., and Briggum, S. M. (1981) Quantitative stylistic analysis of impressionist style in Joseph Conrad and Ford Madox Ford. In: Bailey, R. W. (ed.) *Computing in the humanities. Papers from the fifth international conference on computing in the humanities, Ann Arbor, Michigan, May 1981.* North-Holland, Amsterdam, pp. 59–64.

Bentley, B. (1987) Software for Spanish students: STANCALL and its reception in the classroom. In: Chesters, G. (ed.) *The use of computers in the teaching of language and languages.* Computers in Teaching Initiative Support Service, Bath, pp. 127–138.

Benwell, G. A. (1986) Integrating the computer into a language course. In: Cameron, K. C., Dodd, W. S. and Rahtz, S. P. Q. (eds) *Computers and modern language studies,* Ellis Horwood, Chichester, pp. 15–19.

Berliner, H. J. (1981) Search vs. knowledge: an analysis from the domain of games. In: Elithorn, A., and Banerji, R. (eds) *Artificial and human intelligence* Elsevier, Amsterdam, pp. 105–117.

Bernard, L. (1987) Principles of database design. In: Rahtz, S. (ed.) *Information technology in the humanities: tools techniques and applications.* Ellis Horwood, Chichester, pp. 54–68.

Bisiani, R. (1987) Some considerations on computer architectures for artificial intelligence. In: Haton, J.-P. (ed.) *Fundamentals in computer understanding: speech and vision.* CUP, Cambridge, pp. 61–77.

Bjørn-Andersen, P. (1988) Are 'human factors' human? *Computer Journal* **31**, 386–90.

Blombach, A. K. (1981) Harmony vs. counterpoint in the Bach chorales. In: Bailey, R. W. (ed.) *Computing in the humanities. Papers from the fifth international conference on computing in the humanities, Ann Arbor, Michigan, May 1981.* North-Holland, Amsterdam, pp. 79–88.

Borello, E. (1981) CAI techniques in linguistics. In: Bailey, R. W. (ed.)

Computing in the humanities. Papers from the fifth international conference on computing in the humanities, Ann Arbor, Michigan, May 1981. North-Holland, Amsterdam, pp. 39–40.

Brainerd, B. (1981) The type–token relation in the works of S. Kierkegaard. In: Bailey, R. W. (ed.) *Computing in the humanities. Papers from the fifth international conference on computing in the humanities, Ann Arbor, Michigan, May 1981.* North-Holland, Amsterdam, pp. 97–109.

Brockett, A. (1987) Using the BBC as a back-up to a beginner's course in Arabic. In: Chesters, G. (ed.) *The use of computers in the teaching of language and languages.* Computers in Teaching Initiative Support Service, Bath, pp. 38–44.

Broughton, J. M. (1984) The surrender of control: computer literacy as political socialization of the child. In: Sloan, D. (ed.) *The computer in education: a critical perspective.* Columbia University, New York, pp. 102–122.

Buchanan, B. G. (1982) New research in expert systems. In: Hayes, J. E., Michie, D. and Pao, Y.-H. (eds) *Machine intelligence 10.* Ellis Horwood, Chichester, pp. 269–299.

Burgess, G. A. (1986) The use of the micro in an integrated German language course at university level. In: Cameron, K. C., Dodd, W. S. and Rahtz, S. P. Q. (eds) *Computers and modern language studies.* Ellis Horwood, Chichester, pp. 20–26.

Bush, C. D., and Robertson, J. S. (1981) The microcomputer in linguistic research. In: Bailey, R. W. (ed.) *Computing in the humanities. Papers from the fifth international conference on computing in the humanities, Ann Arbor, Michigan, May 1981.* North-Holland, Amsterdam, pp. 27–31.

Butler, C. (1987) Computational text analysis: a survey in relational to CALL. In: Chesters, G. (ed.) *The use of computers in the teaching of language and languages.* Computers in Teaching Initiative Support Service, Bath, pp. 67–79.

Byte Magazine (1988). In depth section on hypertext, October 1988, pp. 237–268.

Cairns, F., and Haywood, M. (1987) The computerisation of *Learning Latin: an introductory course for adults.* In: Chesters, G. (ed.) *The use of computers in the teaching of language and languages.* Computers in Teaching Initiative Support Service, Bath, pp. 51–54.

Cameron, K. C. (ed.) (1989) *Computer assisted language learning. Program structure and principles.* Blackwell Scientific, Oxford.

Cameron, K. C., Dodd, W. S. and Rahtz, S. P. Q. (eds) (1986) *Computers and modern language studies.* Ellis Horwood, Chichester.

Carroll, J. M. (1985) Minimalist design for active users. In: B. Shakel (ed.) *Human–computer interaction — Interact '84. Proceedings of the IFIP conference.* North-Holland, Amsterdam, pp. 39–44.

Carroll, J. M., and McKendree, Jean (1987) Interface design issues for advice-giving expert systems. *Comm. ACM* **30** (No. 1) 14–31.

Cellérier, G. (1983) Guidance of action by knowledge. In: Groner, R., Groner M., and Bischof, W. F. (eds) *Methods of heuristics.* Lawrence Erlbaum, London, pp. 141–192.

Chesters, G. (ed.) (1987) *The use of computers in the teaching of language and languages.* Computers in Teaching Initiative Support Service, Bath.

Clark, K. L., and McCabe, F. G. (1982) PROLOG: a language for implementing expert systems. In: Hayes, J. E., Michie, D. and Pao, Y.-H. (eds) *Machine intelligence 10.* Ellis Horwood, Chichester, pp. 455–475.

Clarke, D. (1989) Design considerations in writing CALL software with particular reference to extended materials. In: Cameron, K. C. (ed.) *Computer assisted language learning. Program structure and principles.* Blackwell Scientific, Oxford, pp. 28–37.

Claxton, G. (ed.) (1980) *Cognitive psychology: new directions.* Routledge and Kegan Paul, London.

Clocksin, W. F., and Mellish, C. S. (1981) *Programming in Prolog.* Springer, Berlin.

Coleman, J. (ed.) (1987) *The interactive videodisc in language teaching.* Lochee Publications, New Alyth, Perthshire.

Compte, C. (1987) L'enseignement des langues étrangères et le vidéodisc. In: Coleman, J. (ed.) *The interactive videodisc in language teaching.* Lochee Publications, New Alyth, Perthshire pp. 21–49.

Computer Journal (1988) Special issue on the human–computer interface **31** (no. 5).

Conklin, J. (1987) A survey of hypertext. *IEEE Computer,* September 1987.

Cooley, M. (1987) *Architect or bee? The human price of technology.* Hogarth Press, London.

Coombs, M. J., and Alty, J. L. (eds) (1981) *Computing skills and the user interface.* Academic Press, London.

Corns, T. and Smith, M. E. (1987) Literature. In: Rahtz, S. (ed.) *Information technology in the humanities: tools techniques and applications.* Ellis Horwood, Chichester, pp. 104–115.

Crichton, M. (1984) *Electronic life. Understanding the computer age.* Arrow Books, London.

Crookall, D. (1986) CALLS: Computer-Assisted Language Learning Simulation. In: Cameron, K. C., Dodd, W. S. and Rahtz, S. P. Q. (eds) *Computers and modern language studies,* Ellis Horwood, Chichester, pp. 113–121.

Cuffaro, H. K. (1984) Microcomputers in education: why is earlier better? In: Sloan, D. (ed.) (1984) *The computer in education: a critical perspective.* Columbia University, New York, pp. 21–30.

Damodaran, L. (1988) Editorial. *Computer Journal* **31** 385.

Davies, G. (1985) *Using computers in language learning: a teacher's guide.* CILT, London.

Davy, J. (1984) Mindstorms in the lamplight. In: Sloan, D. (ed.) (1984) *The computer in education: a critical perspective.* Columbia University, New York, pp. 11–20.

De Groot, A. D. (1983) Heuristics, mental programs, and intelligence. In: Groner, R., Groner M., and Bischof, W. F. (eds) *Methods of heuristics.* Lawrence Erlbaum, London, pp. 109–130.

Delcourt, C., and Mersch, G. (1981) Cluster analysis and the taxonomy of words in Old French. In: Bailey, R. W. (ed.) *Computing in the humanities. Papers from the fifth international conference on computing in the humanities, Ann Arbor, Michigan, May 1981.* North-Holland, Amsterdam, pp. 111–122.

Delgrande, J.P., and Mylopoulos, J. (1987) Knowledge representation: features of knowledge. In: Haton, J.-P. (ed.) *Fundamentals in computer understanding: speech and vision.* CUP, Cambridge, pp. 23–59.

DeVoto, B. (1950) *The world of fiction.* Houghton Mifflin, Boston.

Diller, K. C. (1978) *The language teaching controversy.* Rowley, Massachusetts.

Dillon, A., McKnight C., and Richardson, J. (1988) Reading from paper versus reading from screen. *Computer Journal* **31** 457–464.

Dörner, D. (1983) Heuristics and cognition in complex systems. In: Groner, R., Groner, M., and Bischof, W. F. (eds) *Methods of heuristics.* Lawrence Erlbaum, London, pp. 89–108.

Dreyfus (1972) *What computers can't do.* Harper and Row, London.

Dreyfus, H. L., and Dreyfus, S. E. (1984) Putting computers in their proper place. In: Sloan, D. (ed.) (1984) *The computer in education: a critical perspective.* Columbia University, New York, pp. 40–63.

Du Boulay, B., and O'Shea, T. O. (1981) Teaching novices programming. In: Coombs, M. J., and Alty, J. L. (eds) *Computing skills and the user interface.* Academic Press, London, pp. 147–200.

Duda, R. O., Hart, P. E., and Nilsson, N. J. (1981) Subjective Bayesian methods for rule-based inference systems. In: Webber, B. L., & Nilsson, N. J. (eds) *Readings in artificial intelligence.* Pal Alto, California, pp. 192–199.

Duranni, O. (1986) Computer applications for final-year linguists. In: Cameron, K. C., Dodd, W. S. and Rahtz, S. P. Q. (eds) *Computers and modern language studies,* Ellis Horwood, Chichester, pp. 27–36.

Durrani, O. (1989) Designer labyrinths: text mazes for language learners. In: Cameron, K. C. (ed.) *Computer assisted language learning. Program structure and principles.* Blackwell Scientific, Oxford, pp. 38–48.

Elithorn, A. and Banerji, R. (eds) (1981) *Artificial and human intelligence.* Elsevier, Amsterdam.

Elithorn, A., Cooper, R., and Telford, A. (1981) Benchmark and yardstick problems: a systematic approach. In: Elithorn, A., and Banerji, R. (eds) *Artificial and human intelligence.* Elsevier, Amsterdam, pp. 201–212.

Elsom-Cook, M. (1985) Design considerations of an intelligent teaching system for programming languages. In: B. Shackel (ed.) *Human–computer interaction — Interact '84. Proceedings of the IFIP Conference.* North-Holland, Amsterdam, pp. 409–413.

Ennals, R. (1987) An historical perspective. In: Rahtz, S. *Information technology in the humanities: tools techniques and applications.* Ellis Horwood, Chichester, pp. 10–19.

Farrington, B. (1981) Computer based learning exercises for language learning at university level. In: Smith, P. R. (ed.). *Computer assisted learning. Selected proceedings from the CAL 81 symposium*, Pergamon, London, 1981, pp. 113–116.

Farrington, B. (1986) Computer assisted learning or computer inhibited acquisition? In: Cameron, K. C., Dodd, W. S., and Rahtz, S. P. Q. (eds) *Computers and modern language studies*, Ellis Horwood, Chichester, pp. 85–92.

Farrington, B. (1989) AI: grandeur or servitude? In: Cameron, K. C. (ed.) *Computer assisted language learning. Program structure and principles.* Blackwell Scientific, Oxford, pp. 67–80.

Feigenbaum, E. A. & McCorduck, P. (1984) *The fifth generation. Artificial intelligence and Japan's computer challenge to the world.* Michael Joseph, London.

Ferney, D. (1989) Small programs that 'know' what they teach. In: Cameron, K. C. (ed.) *Computer assisted language learning. Program structure and principles.* Blackwell Scientific, Oxford, pp. 14–27.

Fiderio, J. (1988) A grand vision. *Byte Magazine* October 1988 237–244.

Fodor, J. A. (1983) *The modularity of mind.* MIT Press, Cambridge, Massachusetts.

Fox, J. (1986) Computer-assisted reading — work in progress at the University of East Anglia. In: Cameron, K. C., Dodd, W. S., and Rahtz, S. P. Q. (eds) *Computers and Modern Language Studies*, Ellis Horwood, Chichester, pp. 70–77.

Fox. J (1989) Can computers aid vocabulary learning?. In: Cameron, K. C. (ed.) *Computer assisted language learning.* Program structure and principles. Blackwell Scientific, Oxford, pp. 1–13.

Frisse, M. (1988) From Text to Hypertext. *Byte Magazine* October 1988 247–254.

Gaines, B. R. (1985) From ergonomics to the fifth generation: 30 years of human–computer interaction studies. In: Shackel, B. (ed.) *Human–computer interaction — Interact '84. Proceedings of the IFIP Conference.* North-Holland, Amsterdam, pp. 3–7.

Galleily, J. E., and Butcher, C. W. (1989) Towards an intelligent syntax checker. In: Cameron, K. C. (ed.) *Computer assisted language learning. Program structure and principles.* Blackwell Scientific, Oxford, pp. 81–100.

Garnham, A. (1988) *Artificial intelligence. An introduction.* Routledge, London.

Garvin, P. L. (1985) The current state of language data processing. In: Yovits, M. C. (ed.) *Advances in computers 24*. London, 1985, pp. 217–275.

Gaschnig, J. G. (1982) Application of the PROSPECTOR system to geological exploration problems. In: Hayes, J. E., Michie, D., and Pao, Y.-H. (eds) *Machine intelligence 10*. Ellis Horwood, Chichester, pp. 301–323.

Geens, D. (1981) Computer-driven remedial teaching of foreign languages. In: Bailey, R. W. (ed.) *Computing in the humanities. Papers from the fifth international conference on computing in the humanities, Ann Arbor, Michigan, May 1981*. North-Holland, Amsterdam, pp. 41–46.

Gevarter, W. (1984) *Artificial intelligence. Expert systems. computer vision and natural language processing*. Park Ridge, New Jersey.

Gleick, J. (1988) *Chaos. Making a new science*. Heinemann, London.

Goldberg, A. & Polil, I. (1981) Is complexity theory of use to AI? In: Elithorn, A., and Banerji, R. (eds) *Artificial and human intelligence*. Elsevier, Amsterdam, pp. 43–55.

Green, C. G., and Westfold, S. J. (1982) Knowledge-based programming self-applied. In: Hayes, J. E., Michie, D., and Pao, Y.-H. *Machine intelligence 10*. Ellis Horwood, Chichester, pp. 325–338.

Griswold, R. E. (1981) The Icon programming language. In: Bailey, R. W. (ed.) *Computing in the humanities. Papers from the fifth international conference on computing in the Humanities, Ann Arbor, Michigan, May 1981*. North-Holland, Amsterdam, pp. 7–17.

Groner, M., Groner, R., and Bischof, W. F. (1983a) Approaches to heuristics: a historical review. In: Groner, R., Groner M., and Bischof, W. F. (eds) *Methods of heuristics*. Lawrence Erlbaum, London, pp. 1–18.

Groner, R., Groner M., and Bischof, W. F. (eds) (1983b) *Methods of Heuristics*. Lawrence Erlbaum, London.

Gummery, P. J., and Crompton, P. M. (1986) Computerized information retrieval system for undergraduates of Spanish. In: Cameron, K. C., Dodd, W. S., and Rahtz, S. P. Q. (eds) *Computers and modern language studies*. Ellis Horwood, Chichester, pp. 136–143.

Gunderson, K. (1985) *Mentality and machines*. Second edition, University of Minnesota Press, Minneapolis.

Halasz, F. G. (1988) Reflections on NoteCards: seven issues for the next generation of hypermidea systems. *Comm. ACM* **31** 836–851.

Hall, W. (1987) The art of programming. In: Rahtz, S. (ed.) *Information technology in the humanities: tools techniques and applications*. Ellis Horwood, Chichester, pp. 80–91.

Halliday, J. (1986) A form of perspective: CALL for Russian. In: Cameron, K. C., Dodd, W. S. and Rahtz, S. P. Q. (eds) *Computers and modern language studies*. Ellis Horwood, Chichester, pp. 52–59.

Hancock, R. (1987) Non-verbal communication on interactive videodisc as an adjunct to language learning. In: Chesters, G. (ed.) *The use of computers in the teaching of language and languages.* Computers in Teaching Initiative Support Service, Bath, p. 99.

Hartley, A. F., and Motley, F. (1986) GRACE — A CALL system for the acquisition of reading skills. In: Cameron, K. C., Dodd, W. S., and Rahtz, S. P. Q. (eds) *Computers and modern language studies.* Ellis Horwood, Chichester, pp. 37–45.

Hasemer, T. (1984) *Looking at LISP.* Addison-Wesley, Reading, Massachusetts.

Haton, J.-P. (ed.) (1987a) *Fundamentals in computer understanding: speech and vision.* CUP, Cambridge.

Haton, J.-P. (1987b) Knowledge-based and expert systems in understanding problems. In: Haton, J.-P. (ed.) *Fundamentals in computer understanding: speech and vision.* CUP, Cambridge, pp. 1–21.

Haugeland, J. (1985) *Artificial intelligence: the very idea.* MIT Press, Cambridge, Massachusetts.

Hayes, J. E. and Michie, D. (eds) (1983) *Intelligent systems,* Ellis Horwood, Chichester.

Hayes, J. E., Michie, D., and Pao, Y.-H. (1982) *Machine intelligence 10.* Ellis Horwood, Chichester.

Hayes-Roth, F., Waterman, D. A., and Lenat, D. B. (eds) (1983) *Building expert systems.* Addison-Wesley, Reading, Massachusetts.

Heath, L. (1987) Can CALL be used communicatively? In: Chesters, G. (ed.) *The use of computers in the teaching of language and languages.* Computers in Teaching Initiative Support Service, Bath, pp. 45–50.

Heather, N. (1987) New technological aids for CAL. In: Rahtz, S. (ed.) *Information technology in the humanities: tools techniques and applications.* Ellis Horwood, Chichester, pp. 41–53.

Hill, B. (1987) Developments in interactive video. In: Coleman, J. (ed.) *The interactive videodisc in language teaching.* Lochee Publications, New Alyth, Perthshire, pp. 51–60.

Hockey, S. M. (1987) An historical perspective. In: Rahtz, S. (ed.) *Information technology in the humanities: tools techniques and applications.* Ellis Horwood, Chichester, pp. 20–30.

Huntsman, J. F. (1981) Language and computer languages. In: Bailey, R. W. (ed.) *Computing in the humanities. Papers from the fifth international conference on computing in the humanities, Ann Arbor, Michigan, May 1981.* North-Holland, Amsterdam, pp. 19–26.

Hutchins, W. J. (1986) *Machine translation: past, present, future.* Ellis Horwood, Chichester.

Hypertext Aberdeen 1988 (1988) *Papers from the Alvey HCI Club interactive learning systems SIG,* University Teaching Centre, Aberdeen.

Inhelder, B. (1983) Guidance of action by knowledge. In: Groner, R., Groner M., and Bischof, W. F. (eds) *Methods of heuristics,* Lawrence Erlbaum, London, pp. 131–140.

Inmos Ltd (1988) *Transputer development system,* Prentice Hall, New York.

Jackson, P. (1986) *Introduction to expert systems.* Addison, W. Wokingham.

Jacobs, G. (1987) Multi-choice questions in computer-assisted language learning. In: Chesters, G. (ed.) *The use of computers in the teaching of language and languages.* Computers in Teaching Initiative Support Service, Bath, pp. 12–25.

Johnston, I. A. (1989) *GIBBER.* PhD thesis, University of Dundee.

Jones, G. (1987) The Eurocentres videodisc. In: Coleman, J. (ed.) *The interactive videodisc in language teaching.* Lochee Publications, New Alyth, Perthshire, pp. 61–91.

Joyce, J. (1981) UNIX aids for composition courses. In: Bailey, R. W. (ed.) *Computing in the humanities. Papers from the fifth international conference on computing in the humanities, Ann Arbor, Michigan, May 1981.* North-Holland, Amsterdam, pp. 33–38.

Kemeny, J. G., and Kurtz, T. E. (1985) *True BASIC.* Addison-Wesley, Reading, Massachusetts.

Klinke, G., Genetet, S., and McDermott, J. (1988) Knowledge acquisition for evaluation systems. *International Journal of Man–Machine Studies* **29** 715–731.

Klix, F. (1983) An evolutionary approach to cognitive processes and creativity in human beings. In: Groner, R., Groner M., and Bischof, W. F. (eds) *Methods of heuristics.* Lawrence Erlbaum, London, pp. 19–36.

Knipers, B. (1987) New reasoning methods for artificial intelligence in medicine. *International Journal of Man–Machine Studies* **26** 707–718.

Kochen, M. (1983) An evolutionary approach to hypothesis and concept formulation. In: Groner, R., Groner M., and Bischof, W. F. (eds) *Methods of heuristics.* Lawrence Erlbaum, London, pp. 37–68.

Kolodner, J. L. (1981) Knowledge-based self-organizing memory for events. In: Elithorn, A., and Banerji, R. (eds) *Artificial and human intelligence.* Elsevier, Amsterdam, pp. 57–66.

Kümmel, P. (1979) *Formalization of natural languages.* Springer-Verlag, Berlin.

Kunst, A. E., and Blank, G. D. (1981) Processing morphology: words and clichés. In: Bailey, R. W. *Computing in the humanities. Papers from the fifth international conference on computing in the humanities, Ann Arbor, Michigan, May 1981.* North-Holland, Amsterdam, pp. 123–132.

Last, R. W. (1970) The computer and the critic. *The Listener* **84** 482–483.

Last, R. W. (1979) The role of computer-assisted learning in modern language teaching. *ALLC Bulletin* **7** 165–171.

Last, R. W. (1982) Le rôle de l'enseignement par ordinateur dans le laboratoire de langues de l'avenir. *Marche Romane* **32** 29–36.

Last, R. W. (1984) *Language teaching and the microcomputer.* Basil Blackwell, Oxford.

Last, R. W. (1986) The potential of AI-related CALL at the sentence level. *Literary and Linguistic Computing* **1** 197–201.

Last, R. W. (1987) Artificial intelligence — the way forward for CALL? In:

Chesters, G. (ed.) *The use of computers in the teaching of language and languages*. Computers in Teaching Initiative Support Service, Bath, pp. 61–66.

Last, R. W., and King, P. K. (1979) The design and implementation of a computer assisted learning package for modern language teaching: a research progress report. *British Journal of Educational Technology* **10** 194–197.

Last, R. W., and Lewis, D. R. (1985) Teaching the micro to talk. *Modern Languages in Scotland* No. 27 157–163.

Lavorel, P. M. (1981) The distributed processing of knowledge and belief in the human brain. In: Elithorn, A. and Banerji, R. (eds) *Artificial and human intelligence*. Elsevier, Amsterdam, pp. 229–238.

Lenat, D. B. (1983) Towards a theory of heuristics. In: Groner, R., Groner M., and Bischof, W. F. (eds) *Methods of heuristics*. Lawrence Erlbaum, London, pp. 351–404.

Lewis, D. R. (1985) The development and progress of machine translation systems. *ALLC Journal* **5** 40–52.

L'Huillier, M. (1986) Analysis of conjugation mistakes in French verbs on a microcomputer. In: Cameron, K. C., Dodd, W. S., and Rahtz, S. P. Q. (eds) *Computers and modern language studies*, Ellis Horwood, Chichester, pp. 78–84.

Lukey, F. J. (1981) Comprehending and debugging computer programs. In: Coombs, M. J., and Alty, J. L. (eds) *Computing skills and the user interface*. Academic Press, London, pp. 201–219.

McCorduck, P. (1979) *Machines who think*. Freeman, San Francisco.

McGregor, J. (1987) Text-based language learning. In: Rahtz, S. (ed.) *Information technology in the humanities: tools techniques and applications*. Ellis Horwood, Chichester, pp. 150–158.

Menosky, J. A. (1984) *Computer literacy and the press*. In: Sloan, D. (ed.) (1984) *The computer in education: a critical perspective*. Columbia University, New York, p. 83.

Mikulich, L. I. (1982). Natural language dialogue systems: a pragmatic approach. In: Hayes, J. E., Michie, D., and Pao, Y.-H. (eds) *Machine intelligence 10*. Ellis Horwood, Chichester, pp. 383–396.

Miller, G. A. (1967) *The psychology of human communication*. Allen Lane, London.

Minsky, M. (1983) Jokes and the logic of the cognitive unconscious. In: Groner, R., Groner M., and Bischof, W. F. (eds) *Methods of heuristics*. Lawrence Erlbaum, London, pp. 171–194.

Mortimore, E. P. (1987) *Amiga programmer's handbook*, Vol. 2, 2nd edn. Sybex, San Francisco.

Nancarrow, P. H. (1981) Processing of ancient Egyptian hieroglyphic texts by computer. In: Bailey, R. W. (ed.) *Computing in the humanities. Papers from the fifth international conference on computing in the humanities, Ann Arbor, Michigan, May 1981*. North-Holland, Amsterdam, pp. 175–184.

Newell, A. F. (1983) The heuristic of George Polya and its relation to artificial intelligence. In: Groner, R., Groner M., and Bischof, W. F. (eds) *Methods of heuristics*. Lawrence Erlbaum, London, pp. 195–244.

Newell, A. F. (1985) Speech — the natural modality for man–machine interaction? In: Shackel, B. (ed.) *Human–computer interaction — Interact '84. Proceedings of the IFIP Conference*. North-Holland, Amsterdam, pp. 231–235.

Newell, A. F., and Simon, H. A. (1972) *Human problem solving*. Prentice Hall, Englewood Cliffs, New Jersey.

Noble, D. (1984) Computer literacy and ideology. In: Sloan, D. (ed.) (1984) *The computer in education: a critical perspective*. Columbia University, New York, pp. 64–76.

Nyns, R. R. (1988) Using a database management language to teach reading skills. *Literary and Linguistic Computing* **3** 237–243.

Oborne, D. J. (1985) *Computers at work. A behavioural approach*. John Wiley, Chichester.

Oborne, D. J. (1987) *Ergonomics at work*. John Wiley, Chichester.

O'Neal, G. (1987) The north west educational computing project: an overview. In: Coleman, J. (ed.) *The interactive videodisc in language teaching*. Lochee Publications, New Alyth, Perthshire, pp. 93–101.

O'Shea, T., and Self, J. (1983) *Learning and teaching with computers. Artificial intelligence in education*. Brighton.

O'Shea, T., *et al.* (1984) Tools for creating intelligent computer tutors. In: Elithorn, A. and Banerji, R. (eds) *Artificial and human intelligence*. Elsevier, Amsterdam, pp. 181–199.

Papert, S. (1980) *Mindstorms. Children, computers and powerful ideas*. Harvester Press, Brighton.

Partridge, D. (1986) *Artificial intelligence: applications in the future of software engineering*. Ellis Horwood, Chichester.

Patton, P. C., and Holoien, R. A. (eds) (1981) *Computing in the humanities*, Gower Publishing, Aldershot.

Pearce, A. (1987). Music teaching and computing. In: Rahtz, S. (ed.) *Information technology in the humanities: tools techniques and applications*. Ellis Horwood, Chichester, pp. 116–125.

Piszcalski, M., and Galler, M. (1981) Computer-aided techniques for understanding performed music. In: Bailey, R. W. (ed.) *Computing in the humanities. Papers from the fifth international conference on computing in the humanities, Ann Arbor, Michigan, May 1981*. North-Holland, Amsterdam, pp. 89–96.

Pohl, I. (1984) A taxonomy for the social implications of computer technology. In: Elithorn, A. and Banerji, R. (eds) *Artificial and human intelligence*. Elsevier, Amsterdam, pp. 289–295.

Potter, R. G. (1981) Reader responses and character syntax. In: Bailey, R. W. (ed.) *Computing in the humanities. Papers from the fifth international conference on computing in the humanities, Ann Arbor, Michigan, May 1981*. North-Holland, Amsterdam, pp. 65–78.

Proceedings of the eleventh international conference on computational linguistics (1986) Coling, Bonn.

Rahtz, S. (ed.) (1987a) *Information technology in the humanities: tools techniques and applications.* Ellis Horwood, Chichester.

Rahtz, S. (1987b) The processing of words. In: Rahtz, S. (ed.) *Information technology in the humanities: tools techniques and applications.* Ellis Horwood, Chichester, pp. 69–79.

Raymond, D. R., and Thompa, F. W. (1988) Hypertext and the Oxford English Dictionary. *Comm. ACM* **31** 871–879.

Reiter, R. (1981) On closed world data bases. In: Webber, B. L., and Nilsson, N. J. (eds) *Readings in artificial intelligence.* Tioga, Palo Alto, California, pp. 119–140.

Reitman, W. R. (1965) *Cognition and thought. An information-processing approach.* John Wiley, New York.

Rich, E. (1976) *Artificial intelligence.* John Wiley, New York.

Richardson, B. (1986) CALL in Italian at the University of Leeds. In: Cameron, K. C., Dodd, W. S., and Rahtz, S. P. Q. (eds) *Computers and modern language studies.* Ellis Horwood: Chichester, pp. 46–51.

Ritchie, G. D. (1980) *Computational grammar. An artificial intelligence approach to linguistic description.* Harvester, Brighton.

Roszack, T. (1986) *The cult of information. The folklore of computers and the true art of thinking.* Lutterworth, Cambridge.

Sabol, C. R. (1981) Focus and attribution in Ford and Conrad. In: Bailey, R. W. (ed.) *Computing in the humanities. Papers from the fifth international conference on computing in the humanities, Ann Arbor, Michigan, May 1981.* North-Holland, Amsterdam, pp. 47–58.

Sardello, R. J. (1984) The technological threat to education. In: Sloan, D. (ed.) (1984) *The computer in education: a critical perspective.* Columbia University, New York, pp. 93–101.

Schlesinger, I. M. (1982) *Steps to language. Toward a theory of native language acquisition.* Hillsdale, New Jersey.

Self, J. (1985) *Microcomputers in education.* Harvester, Brighton.

Shackel, B. (ed.) (1985a) *Human–computer interaction — Interact '84. Proceedings of the IFIP Conference.* Amsterdam.

Shackel, B. (1985b) Designing for people in the age of information. In: B. Shackel (ed.) *Human–computer interaction — Interact '84. Proceedings of the IFIP Conference.* Amsterdam, pp. 9–18.

Sharp, J. A. (1987) *An introduction to distributed and parallel processing.* Blackwell Scientific, Oxford.

Shaw, M. L. G. (1985) Knowledge engineering for expert systems. In: *Human–computer interaction Interact '81. Proceedings of the IFIP Conference,* Amsterdam, pp. 489–493.

Simons, G. (1983) *Are computers alive? Evolution and new life forms.* Harvester, Brighton.

Simons, G. (1988) Evolution of the intelligent machine. NCC, Manchester.

Simpson, B. (1984) Heading for the Ha-Ha. In: Sloan, D. (ed.) (1984) *The computer in education: a critical perspective.* Columbia University, New York, pp. 84–92.

Sloan, D. (ed.) (1984a) *The computer in education: a critical perspective.* Columbia University, New York.

Sloan, D. (1984b) Introduction: On raising critical questions about the computer in education. In: Sloan, D. (ed.) (1984a) *The computer in education: a critical perspective.* Columbia University, New York, pp. 1–9.

Sloman, A. (1984) The structure of the space of possible minds. In: Torrance, S. (ed.) *The minds and the machine.* Ellis Horwood, Chichester, p. 35.

Smith, P. R. (ed.) (1981) *Computer assisted learning. Selected proceedings from the CAL 81 symposium,* Pergamon, Oxford.

Sperandio, J. C., and Scapin, D. L. (1987) Ergonomic aspects of man–machine communications. In: Haton, J.-P. (ed.) *Fundamentals in computer understanding: speech and vision.* Cambridge University Press, Cambridge, 79–90.

Steels, L. (1981) ORBIT: a tool for building AI systems in an object-oriented style. In: Elithorn, A., and Banerji, R. (eds) *Artificial and human intelligence.* Elsevier, Amsterdam, pp. 131–140.

Stuart, D. R. (1986) The potential of computerized interpreting in teaching. In: Cameron, K. C., Dodd, W. S., and Rahtz, S. P. Q. (eds) *Computers and modern language studies.* Ellis Horwood, Chichester, pp. 122–135.

Studnicki, F. (1981) A semantic approach to automated resolving of interdocumental cross-references in legal texts. In: Bailey, R. W. *Computing in the humanities. Papers from the fifth international conference on computing in the humanities, Ann Arbor, Michigan, May 1981.* North-Holland, Amsterdam, pp. 133–148.

Suppes, P. (1983) Heuristics and the axiomatic method. In: Groner, R., Groner M., and Bischof, W. F. (eds) *Methods of heuristics.* Lawrence Erlbaum, London, pp. 79–88.

Sutherland, S. (1987) Are minds simply what brains do? *The Times Higher Education Supplement* 9.10.87 17.

Taylor, M. M. (1981) The bilateral cooperative model of reading: a human paradigm for artificial intelligence. In: Elithorn, A., and Banerji, R. (eds) *Artificial and human intelligence,* Elsevier, Amsterdam, pp. 239–250.

Taylor, O. B., and Harding, D. (1986) Computers in Arabic language teaching. In: Cameron, K. C., Dodd, W. S., and Rahtz, S. P. Q. (eds) *Computers and modern language studies,* Ellis Horwood, Chichester, pp. 60–69.

Tikhomirov, O. K. (1983) Informal heuristic principles of motivation and emotion in human problem solving. In: Groner, R., Groner M., and Bischof, W. F. (eds) *Methods of heuristics.* Lawrence Erlbaum, London, pp. 153–170.

Torrance, S. (ed.) (1984) *The mind and the machine.* Ellis Horwood, Chichester.

Trainor, R. (1987) In: Rahtz, S. *Information technology in the humanities: tools techniques and applications.* Ellis Horwood, Chichester, pp. 31–40.

Tuma, D. T., and Reif, F. (1980) *Problem solving and education: issues in teaching and research.* Erlbaum, Hillsdale, New Jersey.

Turkle, Sherry (1984) *The second self. Computers and the human spirit,* Granada, London.

Turner, R. (1984) *Logics for artificial intelligence.* Ellis Horwood, Chichester.

Van der Waerden, B. L. (1983) Inspiration and thinking in mathematics. In: Groner, R., Groner, M., and Bischof, W. F. (eds) *Methods of heuristics.* Lawrence Erlbaum, London, pp. 69–78.

Van Dyke Parunak, H. (1981) Data base design for Biblical texts. In: Bailey, R. W. (ed.) *Computing in the humanities. Papers from the fifth international conference on computing in the humanities, Ann Arbor, Michigan, May 1981.* North-Holland, Amsterdam, pp. 149–161.

Waite, M., Prata, S. and Martin, D. (1987) *UNIX System V primer.* Howard Sams, Indiana.

Walker, A. (ed.), with McCord, M., Sowa, J. F., and Wilson, W. G. (1987) *Knowledge systems and Prolog. A logical approach to expert systems and natural language processing.* Addison-Wesley, Reading, Massachusetts.

Walsh, V. A. (1981) Computer simulation methodology for archaeology. In: Bailey, R. W. (ed.) *Computing in the humanities. Papers from the fifth international conference on computing in the humanities, Ann Arbor, Michigan, May 1981.* North-Holland, Amsterdam, pp. 163–174.

Wasserman, A. I. (1985) Developing interactive information systems with the user software engineering methodology. In: Shakel, B. (ed.) *Human–computer interaction — Interact '84 Proceedings of the IFIP Conference.* North-Holland, Amsterdam, pp. 611–617.

Webber, B. L., and Nilsson, N. J. (eds) (1981) *Readings in artificial intelligence.* Tioga, Palo Alto, California.

Weizenbaum, J. (1984) *Computer power and human reason. From judgement to calculation.* Penguin, Harmondsworth.

Winograd, T. (1983) *Language as a computer process. Vol. I Syntax.* Reading, Massachusetts.

Wisbey, R. A. (1962) Concordance making by electronic computer: some experiences with the 'Wiener Genesis'. *Modern Languages Review* **52** 161–172.

Wright, L. (1989) Aspects of text storage and text compression in CALL. In: Cameron, K. C. (ed.) *Computer assisted language learning. Program structure and principles.* Blackwell Scientific, Oxford, pp. 49–66.

Yazdani, M. (1986) The ideal teaching machine. In: Cameron, K. C., Dodd, W. S., and Rahtz, S. P. Q. (eds) *Computers and modern language studies,* Ellis Horwood, Chichester, pp. 144–153.

Yazdani, M. (1989) Language tutoring with PROLOG. In: Cameron, K. C.

(ed.) *Computer assisted language learning. Program structure and principles.* Blackwell Scientific, Oxford, pp. 101–111.

Zajonc, A. G. (1984) Computer pedagogy? Questions concerning the new educational technology. In: Sloan, D. (ed.) (1984) *The computer in education: a critical perspective.* Columbia University, New York, pp. 31–39.

Zuboff, S. (1988) *In the age of the smart machine.* Heinemann Professional, Oxford.

Computer software

Choicemaster, Wida Software, 2 Nicholas Gardens, London W5 5YH.

Context, Derek Lewis, LocheeSoft, New Alyth, Perthshire, PH11 8NN.

French Pronouns Program, Rex Last, LocheeSoft, New Alyth, Perthshire, PH11 8NN.

German Sentence Building, Iain Johnston, LocheeSoft, New Alyth, Perthshire, PH11 8NN.

German Strong Verbs, Rex Last, LocheeSoft, New Alyth, Perthshire, PH11 8NN.

Reading and Listening Comprehension, Derek Lewis, LocheeSoft, New Alyth, Perthshire, PH11 8NN.

Storyboard, Wida Software, 2 Nicholas Gardens, London W5 5YH.

Tich-Tack, Primrose Publishing (Cambridge), Vicarage Long Barn, Denham, Bury St. Edmunds, IP29 5EF.

Viewbook. Author, Steve Jefferys, Information Education, Bedford Street, Stoke-on-Trent ST1 4PZ.

Addresses

Athelstan Newsletter
P.O. Box 8025–N
La Jolla, CA 92038–8025
USA

CILT
(Centre for Information on Language Teaching and Research)
Regent's College
Inner Circle
Regent's Park
London, NW1 4NS

Computer-assisted language learning
Queen's Building
University
Exeter EX4 4QH

CTISS
(Computers in Teaching Initiative Support Service)
CTI Centre for Modern Languages
Department of French
The University
Hull, HU6 7RX

NCCALL
(National Centre for Computer-Assisted Language Learning)
Ealing College of Higher Education
Grove House
1 The Grove
London, W5 5DX

The Athelstan Newsletter offers information on all aspects of technology and language learning. CILT has a library of CALL software and publishes Davies (1985). Computer-assisted language learning is a new journal devoted to all aspects of CALL. The CTI Centre in Hull University aims to provide an information service for research work in CALL. NCCALL plays a similar role in the public sector, and now publishes CALLBOARD.

Index

DATE DUE

Demco, Inc. 38-293